THE CURE THAT WORKS

The Cure
That Works

**How to Have the World's
Best Healthcare—at a
Quarter of the Price**

Sean Masaki Flynn, PhD

**REGNERY
PUBLISHING**
A Division of Salem Media Group

Regnery® is a registered trademark of Salem Communications Holding Corporation

Cataloging-in-Publication data on file with the Library of Congress

ISBN 978-1-62157-953-3
ebook ISBN 978-1-62157-962-5

Published in the United States by
Regnery Publishing
A Division of Salem Media Group
300 New Jersey Ave NW
Washington, DC 20001
www.Regnery.com

Manufactured in the United States of America

10 9 8 7 6 5 4 3 2 1

Books are available in quantity for promotional or premium use. For information on discounts and terms, please visit our website: www.Regnery.com.

To Rupali Chadha, Marion Mass, Christine L. Saba, Marlene Wust-Smith, Marcy Zwelling, and the many thousands of their fellow physicians who are leading the fight in Washington and in our state capitals against the cronyism and insider dealing that dominate our healthcare system.

CONTENTS

Introduction

I've got great news. In fact, I've got such great news that most people's first reaction is going to be total and utter disbelief.

Most people can't imagine that another country has used forgotten American ideas to not only deliver the world's best healthcare, but deliver it for *75 percent less* than what Americans pay for healthcare now. Even more unimaginable is the fact that this other country ensures that *every* resident has access to the *same* high-quality care. This country does not put the elderly, the poor, or veterans into inferior systems as America does. Everyone participates in the same health insurance system. Everyone receives universal coverage. Everyone—rich or poor, young or old, perfectly healthy or burdened with preexisting conditions—has access to the same providers.

People sink even *further* into disbelief when I explain that everything this other country is doing was not only invented here in the United States but has also been demonstrated to work equally well here in America by local and state governments, as well as by major private employers.

History shows how the pressures of World War II placed the United States on a trajectory of soaring healthcare costs and unequal healthcare access. But we don't have to stay on that lousy trajectory. We can switch to what *actually works*. We can switch to what we ourselves invented. We would not only deliver equal access to quality healthcare; we would also save 75 percent on healthcare costs *system-wide*.

We currently spend about 18 percent of national income on healthcare.[1] If we reduced costs by 75 percent, then we would free up about 13 percent of national income every year. To put that "13 percent of national income" in perspective, consider that annual Social Security spending amounts to only 5 percent of national income; the annual defense budget amounts to only 4 percent of national income; and it would take only 1 percent of national income to bring the Social Security system into long-run actuarial balance so we could keep our promises to seniors.[2]

Pause for a moment and consider the following: If we had just fixed our healthcare system and slashed its costs by 13 percent of national income, what would *you* want to do with the savings? Here are my suggestions. We could take 1 percentage point out of the 13 to fix Social Security; take another 4 percentage points to balance the federal budget deficit; and then still have 8 percentage points of national income—*about $1.6 trillion per year*—to spend on other things, like improving our schools, strengthening our infrastructure, and paying off our national debt.

My plan would also bring back millions of high-paying manufacturing jobs. Right now, General Motors estimates that the total of its annual healthcare spending amounts to $2,000 per vehicle produced by the company. If we cut healthcare costs by 75 percent, General

Motors could slash the price of a new car by $1,500 (75 percent of $2,000). That's the kind of savings that would allow American manufacturing firms to seriously compete against low-wage foreign competition. It's the kind of savings that would bring back millions of high-paying manufacturing jobs.

The benefits of fixing our broken healthcare system would extend far beyong manufacturing. Our hideously costly healthcare system has slashed take-home pay in every sector of the economy. Productivity growth that otherwise would have flowed into workers' paychecks was instead misdirected into our healthcare system as employers struggled to keep up with soaring health insurance premiums.

My plan would solve that problem by making healthcare costs plummet by 75 percent. Health insurance costs would plummet too, and as a result, take-home pay and savings would soar. The benefits would be remarkable.

This book tells the story of how we lost our way and how we can find it again. It is the story of how we can deliver the world's best healthcare for 75 percent less. It is a guide for reforming America's healthcare system with successful, time-tested, all-American principles.

I hope you will read carefully and then share with your friends. Together, we can deliver the world's best healthcare to every American at the world's lowest cost.

Chapter 1

The Cabbie's Tale

I was on a private fact-finding trip. I had come halfway around the world on my own time, on my own dime. I was in Singapore seeking confirmation.

The statistics I'd read hadn't quite convinced me. They indicated that Singapore was delivering the world's best healthcare at the world's lowest costs. But to a cynical economist like myself, that combination of "the world's best healthcare at the world's lowest costs" seemed way too good to be true. So, I'd flown nineteen hours from LAX to examine Singapore's healthcare system in person.

I wanted answers that I couldn't get from columns of numbers glowing on a computer screen. I wanted confirmation that the statistics weren't lying. I wanted to know if the outcomes were really *that* good and the costs really *that* low. And I wanted to know if what they were doing might also work back home in the United States.

I brought enough money to stay for a week, and I asked one local after another what they thought of Singapore's healthcare system. I asked medical doctors, dentists, and nurses. I asked former public health officials. And I asked virtually every taxi driver, shoeshine boy, waiter, and shop clerk I happened to meet.

On the third day, I was in a cab heading back to the Central Business District after visiting a government-run polyclinic. I had chosen this specific clinic because it was located in one of Singapore's poorest neighborhoods. I wanted to see what public healthcare was like in one of the poorest places in the country.

I had been impressed. The three-story clinic was modern, clean, and efficient. People in the neighborhood could drop by to obtain nearly every outpatient service imaginable, including urgent care and physical therapy. There was also a pharmacy, so prescriptions could be filled immediately on site. Major surgeries and trauma cases were assigned to hospitals, but the neighborhood polyclinic could provide care for just about everything else.

I left after a senior nurse at the polyclinic asked me to stop taking photographs. I can understand why my behavior seemed out of place; she couldn't understand why anybody would be impressed by her polyclinic. She was used to it, as were the patients. I didn't explain that I wanted to take pictures to show people back home how well everything was run. I simply apologized, shook her hand, and grabbed a taxi back to my hotel.

The next fifteen minutes were a revelation. My cabbie was about fifty-five-years-old, of medium build, and as chatty as your favorite uncle. He was of Chinese ethnicity, as is 70 percent of Singapore's population. We talked about local politics, rugby, and finally, healthcare.

I asked him directly: "What do you think about Singapore's healthcare system?"

"I hate it!" was his immediate reply.

I was in the back seat and he couldn't see my face, but I'm sure I looked more than a little surprised. I had been in Singapore three days, and everything I'd seen of its healthcare system had lived up to the hype. But maybe this cabbie knew of some flaws that weren't obvious to outsiders.

I kept my voice level, so as to indicate neither agreement nor disagreement. I asked him: "Why?"

"Because I have to go to the gym three days a week!" he explained, evidently exasperated.

"Does the government force you to do that?"

"No. But if I get fat and get diabetes, I am going to have to pay for a lot of the costs. So I have to go to the gym three times a week."

In the back seat, I smiled. What he was describing was not a problem. It was an answer. Back home, there was much discussion among healthcare professionals about how to get people to exercise, eat better, and take preventive actions to improve their health and well-being. But it was mostly just talk. Nobody back in the States had figured out a way to get people to put in the consistent effort necessary for maintaining health over the long run.

The answer to that dilemma was staring me in the face. I was speaking to an average guy, with an average job, making average money, who possessed an average education. He was telling me that his healthcare system motivated him to get off his butt and exercise three times a week. He was complaining, but I was grinning. What he described as a problem was actually a solution. What he described as a bug was actually a feature. What he disliked about Singapore's healthcare system was something that I instantly wanted to prescribe for the United States.

As the week went on, I continued to encounter more and more aspects of their healthcare system that I wanted to prescribe for ours—things like consumer choice, provider accountability, and a comprehensive safety net. Everything I saw at clinics, hospitals, and in conversations with average people led me to the same conclusion:

the statistics were right. The hype was deserved. Singapore had truly built the world's highest-quality, lowest-cost healthcare system.

After I flew home, I was in for another shock. I discovered that every major component of Singapore's healthcare system—things like price tags and health savings accounts—were *originally developed in the United States*, in many cases decades earlier. That meant that *we* should have been the first country to deliver the world's highest quality, lowest cost healthcare. But we merely invented, while Singapore implemented.

The result? Singapore was delivering the world's best health outcomes while spending 75 percent less per person on healthcare than the United States, and 50 to 60 percent less than countries like Canada and the United Kingdom that are often suggested as models for US healthcare reform.

The international comparisons became even more shocking when I saw just how high Singapore ranks in terms of healthcare quality. Singapore is the only country in the world that can boast of a top-five ranking in each of the three most important measures of healthcare effectiveness. Singapore ranks third in life expectancy, fourth in infant mortality, and first in maternal mortality.[1] By contrast, the United States ranks forty-second in life expectancy, fifty-sixth in infant mortality, and forty-seventh in maternal mortality. Compared with Singapore, Americans die five years earlier, endure an infant mortality rate nearly two-and-a-half times higher, and mourn mothers dying in childbirth six times as frequently.[2]

The performance of the US healthcare system remains dismal even if you take a broader view by including other measures of healthcare effectiveness. *Bloomberg Businessweek* used twenty-one healthcare measures to create a ranking of the world's healthiest countries, including not only life expectancy and infant mortality but also death rates from communicable and non-communicable diseases, HIV infection rates, tobacco usage, obesity rates, environmental pollution rates, immunization rates, total cholesterol levels, alcohol consumption, and the degree of physical activity in which people engage.[3] *Bloomberg*'s conclusion after comparing 145 countries? Singapore ranks *number one* as the world's healthiest country. By contrast, the United States ranks thirty-third, behind not only developed nations such as Japan, the United Kingdom, and Canada, but also much poorer countries such as Greece, Portugal, Costa Rica, Chile, and Cuba.

Our poor performance is disgraceful. But it becomes downright infuriating when you realize that we are spending nearly three times as much per person as Singapore. And it is a national embarrassment that Singapore's system is based on policies that we ourselves invented.

In fact, everything Singapore has implemented has been shown to work just as well here in the United States, both by private companies like Whole Foods Market and by state and local governments. Leaders like Whole Foods founder John Mackey and former Indiana governors Mitch Daniels and Mike Pence have shown that we don't have to continue with business as usual. We can implement; we can join Singapore in delivering the world's best healthcare at the world's lowest costs.

The benefits would be enormous. We would free up enough money each year to fix Social Security, balance the budget, and still have trillions left over to spend on other important priorities like education and national defense. The drastically lower healthcare costs would also slash production costs and make domestic manufacturers competitive on international markets again. We would regain millions of the high-paying manufacturing jobs that have been lost over the past generation.

But if you sign on to implement this better reality, don't expect any thanks; a few years after it's done, Americans probably won't even remember how bad things were, or notice how great the new system is. In the same way that a fish doesn't know that it's living in water, most people won't know they're living in and benefiting from the world's most amazing healthcare system. As with my cabbie in Singapore, people will find things to complain about. But every one of our lives is at stake as well as trillions of dollars that could be devoted to other priorities, such as education and infrastructure. So while reform will probably be thankless, it won't be fruitless.

If we can just implement what we invented, we can live longer, stronger lives while also enjoying a thriving economy, higher take-home pay, a solvent Social Security system, and the peace of mind that will come with knowing that everyone in America has access to the world's best healthcare at the world's lowest prices.

Chapter 2

Singapore Past and Present

The data in Chapter 3 will demonstrate how Singapore's health-care system is world-class in respect to outcomes and costs. But to put those achievements in context, let me first give a brief synopsis of Singapore's economic, social, and political history.

THE COLONY OF SINGAPORE

Singapore lies at the southern end of Indochina, along a highly important maritime trade route (see Figure 2.1). It became a British colony in 1819, when Sir Thomas Stamford Raffles signed a treaty on behalf of the British East India Company with the local Malay ruler, Sultan Hussein Shan. When Raffles took possession of Singapore, there were perhaps one thousand Malays and a handful of ethnic Chinese living on the island. The British East India Company soon established rubber plantations and brought in mostly Chinese laborers (as well as some Indians) to work on the plantations. By 1870, the population had reached almost eighty-five thousand people. Over half were Chinese, and the majority of them were from China's coastal Fujian province.

Figure 2.1: Location of Singapore in Asia

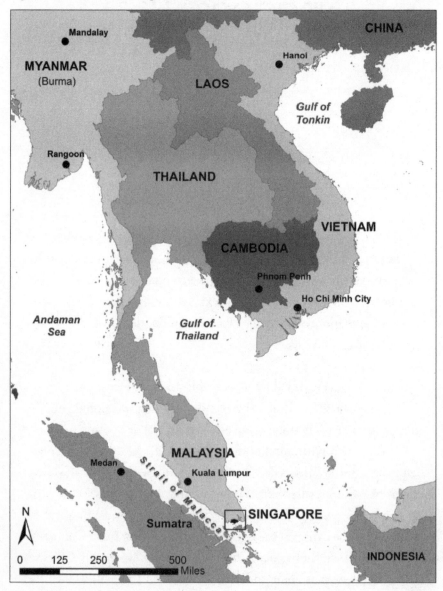

As time passed, Singapore became a major hub for the processing and exporting of locally grown rubber, as well as rubber grown throughout the rest of Southeast Asia. Singapore's location at the tip of the Malay Peninsula and the southern end of the Strait of Malacca meant it was well positioned to serve these industries. The Strait of Malacca runs southeasterly for five hundred miles between the Malay Peninsula and the Indonesian island of Sumatra. It was, and remains, one of the great choke points of world trade, a five-hundred-mile funnel that provides the fastest route for any ship sailing east-west through Asia.

For centuries, the Strait of Malacca served as the seafarer's Silk Road. Singapore's location at its more economically vibrant southern end made it the natural location for traders from East and West to meet and exchange goods. Thus, Singapore quickly developed as a trading port and meeting place, with goods from the West exchanged for products from the East. Rubber still mattered, but the local economy was soon dominated by long-distance trade.

Singapore remained a British colony and was administered as part of India until 1963. It then became part of newly independent Malaysia for two years, before becoming an independent nation in 1965. At that time, Singapore was quite poor. In 1965 its gross domestic product (GDP) per person in US dollars was just $4,754—and that's after adjusting for Singapore's then lower cost of living. By comparison, US GDP per person was $23,918 that year, meaning Singapore's standard of living was 80 percent lower than the United States' standard of living.

But Singapore then embarked on the longest, fastest, and most enduring burst of economic growth in world history. By 2013, its GDP per person—in 2013 US dollars—was $62,400 (after adjusting for Singapore's now higher cost of living). By comparison, the US figure for that year was just $52,800. In just forty-eight years,

Singapore went from being 80 percent poorer than the United States to being almost 20 percent richer. It had transformed itself from a third-world trading post into the world's seventh richest nation.

The only countries that could boast of a higher GDP per capita that year—Qatar, Liechtenstein, Macau, Bermuda, Monaco, and Luxembourg—were all either international banking havens, gambling destinations, or drowning in oil money. Among nations with diversified economies, Singapore was the world's richest country.

RICH, GREEN, AND PROSPEROUS

The health of Singapore's citizens improved just as dramatically as their standard of living. At the time of independence, infectious diseases like cholera, typhoid, and yellow fever were still a threat. Nutrition was poor, raw sewage flowed directly into rivers and ports, and factories dumped toxic waste into local waterways without any legal repercussions. Today, Singapore is clean, modern, and healthy. The rivers and ports are pristine, the city is crisscrossed with greenbelts, and the environmental laws are rigorous. In fact, Singapore is ranked as Asia's greenest (most environmentally pristine) city by the Economist Intelligence Unit and as the world's greenest city (having the highest density of tree cover) by MIT's Green View Index.[1]

Singapore's human environment is vibrant, too, with its multiethnic society serving as a model of cultural synergy and racial harmony. Its residents can boast about having one of the world's top ports, two world-class universities, a superb public transportation system, and an economy that enables 93 percent of its citizens to own their own homes. (By comparison, homeownership in the United States runs at only 65 percent.)

A key point is that Singapore's economy allows its citizens not only to prosper, but to become truly rich. It held the top spot in both

2010 and 2011 for the highest percentage of millionaire households in the world. Even after it slipped down to third place in 2013, fully 10 percent of its households had enough accumulated wealth to rank as millionaire households (in US dollars).[2] Only oil-rich Qatar and banking-haven Switzerland could boast higher percentages. Among nations with diversified economies, Singapore is among the best at catapulting its citizens to millionaire status.

HOW DID THINGS GET SO GOOD?

How did Singapore get from *there* to *here*? How did it climb from Third World to First in just fifty short years?

The simple answer is good governance. Under the leadership of Prime Minister Lee Kuan Yew, Singapore's government set out to find and implement whatever policies were consistent with high rates of growth, rapid improvements in environmental quality, and human flourishing.

Born in 1923, Prime Minister Lee was the leader of the People's Action Party (PAP) from before independence until his retirement in 1990. As the head of the PAP, he was first elected prime minister when the British granted Singapore home rule (but not full independence) in 1959. When independence came in 1963, he helped broker a federation with Malaysia—but after Chinese-Malay race riots flared in 1964, Malaysia decided to expel Singapore. As a result, Lee became the prime minister of a fully independent nation in 1965.

That may sound grand, but Singapore possessed little more than its independence. It depended on Malaysia for much of its water. It had very limited defensive capabilities and almost no natural resources. And it was a tiny island of less than 276 square miles, populated by fewer than two million residents. By way of comparison, the five boroughs that make up New York City are 305 square miles in area and, in 1965, were home to 7.8 million people.

Lee was undaunted. He believed firmly that Singapore could become a first-world nation, and he was in a unique position to make that dream a reality. At the time, the PAP was extremely popular, winning most elections by 70 percent or more. With that level of popular support, Lee did not have to cater to special interests, the whims of opposition parties, or even to disgruntled members of his own party. He was free to pursue whatever economic, social, and environmental policies he thought best as he built up the small island nation (see Figure 2.2).

Figure 2.2: National Map of Singapore

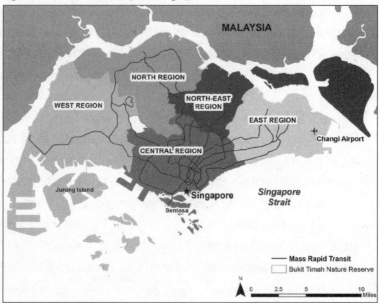

Over the coming decades, the ongoing success of Lee's policies made the PAP overwhelmingly popular, thereby extending Lee's ability to continue his implementations. To this day, the PAP wins elections by wide majorities. These near-certain victories allow the government to take the long view. Government ministers can spend their terms of office focused on solving problems, rather than on getting reelected.

POLICIES FOR PROSPERITY?

So what policies did Lee actually pursue? First and foremost, he sought to make Singapore a meritocracy by providing world-class schools and promoting only the brightest and most accomplished graduates to government administrative positions. This helped to ease racial tensions, as children from all ethnicities and religious groups were presented with an equal chance at advancement. The high quality of Singapore's schools also provided a constant stream of highly educated graduates who were immediately capable of moving into scientific research, highly skilled professions, and business.

Today, Singapore's K–12 students take first place each year on the worldwide academic rankings compiled by the Organization for Economic Cooperation and Development's Programme for International Student Assessment, while also placing in the top three every year in The Learning Curve rankings of international student achievement (compiled by the Economist Intelligence Unit).[3] In fact, academic achievement is so high that 93 percent of Singapore's high school students take calculus before graduating.[4] In the United States that figure is just 16 percent.[5]

Lee then went about providing affordable modern housing, even to the poor. The government's Housing and Development Board subsidized the construction of hundreds of thousands of apartment buildings and then sold them—as opposed to renting them—to the masses. Lee believed firmly that home ownership gave people a real stake in the economy and a reliable vehicle for long-term savings. The Housing and Development Board also went out if its way to prevent any ethnic group from becoming geographically isolated or ghettoized by using quotas to make sure every apartment building and every neighborhood was integrated both racially and religiously. By living together as neighbors and sending their children to the same neighborhood schools, Singaporeans of all backgrounds could feel a deep sense of equality of opportunity.

Lee's next step was to foster industrial growth. He doggedly pursued this goal along several different lines. First, he encouraged business owners to upgrade to factories with better technologies in order to increase productivity. This helped Singapore avoid the "middle-income trap" that befalls many nations as they attempt to industrialize. Countries that fall victim to the middle-income trap initially find economic development to be straightforward, as they transition fairly easily from agriculture and resource extraction to light industries, such as textile manufacturing. As they transition, their living standards rise from poor to lower-middle class, and the population begins to shift from rural to urban. That's nice; however, nations then often get stuck at this sweatshop level of industrialization, unable to develop heavy industries, let alone high-tech industries or a cutting-edge service sector. They lack the incentives to make the necessary investments in education and technology that would lead to higher levels of technological sophistication, productive efficiency, and living standards.

How did Lee avoid this "middle-income trap"? He offered light-industry factory owners both a carrot and a stick. The carrot came by way of heavy government subsidies for purchasing higher-tech equipment (and training workers to use it). The stick was a surtax on wages. For example, it remained perfectly legal for a clothing manufacturer to reject the subsidies and keep on with his low-productivity factory. And it remained perfectly legal for him to keep paying his workers sweatshop wages (e.g., 25 cents per hour). But if the manufacturer went that route, the government would come in and demand that it also receive 25 cents per hour, thereby boosting the company's cost of labor from 25 cents per hour to 50 cents per hour. By raising the cost of labor in this manner, the government whacked manufacturers with a stick. Their low-productivity, low-tech factories would no longer be profitable; they would be better off taking the subsidies and upgrading. In this way, Singapore got its manufacturing sector safely past the middle-income trap. Singapore's firms have continued to adopt higher levels of technology, which has raised both productivity and wages.

As you might expect, this process was greatly assisted by the deluge of well-educated workers pouring out of Singapore's excellent schools. With so many well-educated workers, firms could easily and repeatedly upgrade to more sophisticated production methods. Today, Singapore's manufacturers are among the world's best in high-tech efficiency and innovation, and its universities have become leading centers for cutting-edge scientific research.

SAVINGS AND WEALTH

A compulsory savings scheme, known as the Central Provident Fund (CPF), also helped to modernize Singapore. Established in 1955 by the British, the fund created a mandatory retirement savings account for each worker and forced both the worker and his employer to contribute to the account. Initially, the employee and the employer contributed 5 percent each into the employee's CPF account (for a total of 10 percent). Lee gradually raised contribution rates until they peaked at 25 percent each in 1985. That combined total of 50 percent meant that workers making $40,000 per year would see $20,000 per year put into their CPF savings account.

Fifty percent is a massively high individual savings rate, far higher than anything the United States, Western Europe, or Japan has ever achieved.[6] In fact, since 1959, the United States has never seen its personal savings rate go higher than 17 percent. And over the past twenty-five years, the US personal savings rate has averaged just 5 percent.

The influx of cash generated by the CPF was essential for Singapore's development. It could be used to fund investments in the country's infrastructure, schools, and businesses. Unlike many poor nations forced to borrow billions of dollars from fickle foreign investors, Singapore saved up a massive nest egg of domestic capital ready to be invested in making its economy grow.

But somebody still had to make the right investment decisions. Lee took charge of that, too. He saw that control of the CPF was too important to be handed over to bankers and financiers, who might be tempted to try to maximize short-run profits rather than long-run prosperity. Instead, he appointed engineers and technocrats to oversee the CPF's investments. They favored productive technologies, infrastructure, and education. Because the CPF was so well-funded and grew so much each year, the government always had plenty of money to invest in productive ventures.

Lee also sought to make Singapore attractive to foreign investors. To that end, he established a strong currency fully backed by international assets (which, because they are denominated in foreign currencies, are immune to any changes in Singapore's exchange rate or economic conditions). Lee also ensured that the courts were fair and impartial to foreigners and that property rights were strong and easily enforced.

In fact, Singapore was not merely attractive to foreigners as an investment opportunity. Foreigners with high levels of education or special skills also relocated to Singapore to obtain Singaporean citizenship. Their transition was eased by the fact that as a former British colony, Singapore's government, schools, and business community operated in English.

Finally, taxes were kept low to attract foreign investment and allow local companies to reinvest more of their profits. Today, the highest marginal income tax rate for individuals stands at only 20 percent, while the corporate income tax rate stands at just 17 percent. By way of comparison, the top individual income tax rate in the United States is 37 percent. And until the US corporate tax rate was lowered to 21 percent in 2018, it had been set for decades at 35 percent, the highest of any developed economy and the third highest of all the world's economies.[7]

Singapore's tax system is simple and transparent. It's a flat-tax system with almost no loopholes or deductions available to reduce the amount of taxable income. In fact, the only way for businesses to reduce their taxable incomes is to engage in innovation, investment, or entrepreneurship. Start-ups receive a discount for their first three years of operation. The Productivity and Innovation Credit (PIC) Scheme, introduced in 2010, awards tax credits for research and development (R&D) expenditures, employee training, the purchase or lease of high-efficiency factory equipment, and the acquisition or creation of intellectual property such as patents and copyrights on books, music, and software. The credits are very generous, reaching up to 400 percent of the amounts spent by firms on qualifying activities. As a result, the government presents firms with a massive incentive to innovate, invest, and compete on the world stage.

Singapore's approach to healthcare has been just as supportive of innovation, investment, and efficiency. Its medical institutions can provide high-quality care at low prices precisely because they've adopted the best innovations from around the world and have put policies in place that encourage patients, doctors, and hospitals to increase efficiency, improve outcomes, and resist wasteful spending.

Singapore's innovation-promoting policy stance seems likely to continue. The PAP is still dominant, and although Lee Kuan Yew passed away in 2015, the institutions he fostered remain strong. His eldest son, Lee Hsien Loong, has been Singapore's prime minister since 2004, and it seems more than likely that the elder Lee's preference for innovation, savings, and growth will persist for many years to come.

Chapter 3

Singapore's Healthcare Supremacy

N ow that we've learned more about Singapore's history, let's go over the facts that prove Singapore has created the world's best healthcare system. Two things stand out. The first is that Singapore's healthcare system is world-class in terms of successful outcomes. The second is that it is peerless in terms of low costs.

WORLD-CLASS OUTCOMES

Let's begin with those world-class outcomes. Table 3.1 presents data on life expectancy at birth, the infant mortality rate, and the maternal mortality rate for Singapore, the United States, and several other countries for comparison, as well as the average for the thirty-four nations that are members of the Organization for Economic Cooperation and Development (OECD). (The data for the individual countries comes from the Central Intelligence Agency's online publication, *The World Factbook*, while the data for the OECD comes from the OECD itself.)

As you examine Table 3.1, keep in mind that thirty-one of the thirty-four OECD nations are considered high-income. So the OECD averages shown in the bottom row serve as a benchmark against which we can assess Singapore and the United States, both of which are high-income nations.

Table 3.1: Life Expectancy, Infant Mortality, and Maternal Mortality in Selected Countries, Plus OECD Average

	Life Expectancy at Birth, Years	Infant Mortality Rate per 1,000 Live Births	Maternal Mortality Rate per 100,000 Live Births
Singapore	85.2	2.4	2.4
United States	80.0	5.8	14.0
Canada	81.9	4.5	7.0
United Kingdom	80.8	4.3	9.0
France	81.9	3.2	9.0
Japan	85.3	2.0	6.0
Sweden	82.1	2.6	4.0
Mexico	76.1	11.6	39.0
China	75.7	12.0	28.0
India	68.8	39.1	181.0
OECD Average	80.6	5.5	8.7

Sources: The World Factbook, Central Intelligence Agency, 2018, https://www.cia.gov/library/publications/the-world-factbook/index.html; Government of Singapore, data.gov.sg; OECD Data, https://data.oecd.org; and World Health Organization, Global Health Observatory, http://www.who.int/gho/database/en/. The data for life expectancy are for 2017 (from Central Intelligence Agency and the OECD). The data for infant mortality are for 2015 (from World Health Organization, the OECD, and the Singapore Ministry of Health). The data for maternal mortality are from 2014 (from the World Bank and the OECD).

Beginning with the first column of numbers, we see life expectancy at birth for each country. Only Japan's life expectancy of 85.3 years can beat that of Singapore, and just barely—a tenth of a year translates to just over five weeks. Note also that life expectancy in

Singapore is more than five *years* longer than life expectancy in the United States. That is a large gap. I, for one, would love to live an extra five years.

At the same time, economically impoverished India has a life expectancy of 68.8 years. This is embarrassing for the United States; India spent an average of only $238 per person on health care in 2015, according to World Bank data that adjusts for international differences in purchasing power.[1] Meanwhile, US healthcare spending for 2015 averaged $9,536 per person. Spending $9,298 more than India, per person, per year, only earns US residents an extra eleven years of life expectancy. Clearly, the US is not getting a lot of longevity bang for its healthcare buck.

We can gauge America's dismal rate of return on its healthcare spending still further by comparing the United States with the poorest nation in the Western Hemisphere, Haiti. Haiti has a life expectancy of 63.1 years and spent an average of only $120 dollars per person on healthcare in 2015. What does that mean? It means that Haiti proves you can get 63.1 years of life expectancy while spending next to nothing.

Looking at these facts, a policy-maker might ask herself: *"Well, maybe we should think of this in terms of costs and benefits. Life expectancy is about seventeen years longer in the United States compared to Haiti. But the average lifetime healthcare bill for a US citizen totals a staggering $762,880 ($9,536 per year times 80.0 years of life expectancy) while the average lifetime healthcare bill for a Haitian citizen totals just $7,572 ($120 per year times 63.1 years of life expectancy.) Comparing those two numbers, do we believe that an additional seventeen years of life expectancy is worth spending an additional $755,308 per person?"*

But any policy-maker asking herself that question would miss the real action because that question presents a false dichotomy between spending too much for mediocre results (United States) or spending too little on the way to an early grave (Haiti). Instead, policy-makers should be asking questions like: *"How much are Japan and Singapore spending each year on healthcare as the world leaders in life expectancy? Can we achieve their longer life expectancies while spending less than we do now? Can we live longer while spending less money?"*

ADDRESSING THE REAL QUESTIONS

When our hypothetical policy-maker goes looking for an answer to the first question, he will find that in 2015, Japan spent $4,405 per person on healthcare while Singapore spent just $3,681. The average American will die five years sooner than the average Japanese or Singaporean, *despite* the US spending *more than twice as much* on healthcare per person as Japan and *more than three times as much* per person as Singapore.

Now, it is important to note that Table 3.1 does not contain every country in the world. If you were to look at *The World Factbook's* life expectancy data for *all* the world's nations, you would find that Singapore is ranked third—behind Monaco and Japan, and just ahead of Macau. But Monaco and Macau are tiny nations with a disproportionately high number of extremely wealthy people due to heavy concentrations of gambling and the sort of off-shore banking institutions that help with international tax avoidance.

Because these highly-specialized microstates have very peculiar economies and demographics, it seems sensible to exclude them when it comes to healthcare rankings. But since there are no data sets listing which small countries are the most prone to attracting rich, older people seeking tax havens, let's instead follow a common practice among economic researchers and exclude all countries that have populations of fewer than one million people (sorry, Iceland).

Applying that rule to the life expectancy rankings eliminates Monaco and Macao, thereby leaving Singapore in second place behind Japan among nations with diversified economies and normal demographics. That means that Singapore achieves second place in life expectancy while spending less than any other developed nation on healthcare. And, because its average life expectancy is only five weeks less than Japan's, Singapore is the clear number one when it comes to life expectancy "bang for the buck."

We can use the data in the first column of Table 3.1 to grasp in yet another way just how insanely expensive the US healthcare system is. An OECD country's average life expectancy is 80.6 years, about seven months longer than the US life expectancy of eighty years. But according to the World Bank, the OECD countries' 2015 healthcare spending averaged only $4,887. That's about half of what the US spent on healthcare that year. Consequently, it's not just that the United States looks awful when compared to Singapore; it also looks awful when compared to other rich nations in general. We spend twice as much as the average rich country and die seven months earlier. That level of waste might seem funny if it weren't literally a matter of life and death. With that in mind, let's turn to the data that deals with just about the least funny subject imaginable—the infant mortality rate.

The second column in Table 3.1 provides the 2017 infant mortality rate for each of our comparison countries and for the OECD countries as a group. The infant mortality rate measures how many children die before their first birthdays for every 1,000 children who are born alive in a given year. Among the countries listed in Table 3.1, only Japan outranks Singapore. More importantly for our purposes, the US infant mortality rate of 5.8 is nearly two and a half times greater than Singapore's rate of 2.4 infant deaths per 1,000 live births.

To put that difference in proper perspective, imagine that you or your partner were currently expecting your first child. Would you be happy to find out that your child will be nearly 2.5 times more likely to die before his or her first birthday than a baby born in Singapore? My guess is that you would be horrified to hear that. And your horror would multiply once you discovered that we spend 160 percent more per person on healthcare than Singapore. Surely by spending so much more, infants in the United States wouldn't be 2.5 times more likely to die? Yet, shamefully, they are. That's how wasteful, inefficient, and ineffective our healthcare system is. It kills children.

It also kills mothers, as can be seen in the third column of Table 3.1. In 2015, only 2.4 Singaporean mothers died per 100,000 live births. The US figure that year was 14.0 per 100,000—nearly six times higher than in Singapore. If I were an expecting mother, I'd rather give birth in Singapore—wouldn't you?

In fact, Singapore outranks *all but three* of the world's nations with more than one million people. Only Slovenia, Finland, and Japan can beat Singapore when it comes to maternal mortality.

CONSISTENT EXCELLENCE

The big takeaway from Table 3.1 is that Singapore runs the world's best healthcare system while also spending the least money of any developed nation. It ranks second in life expectancy, second in infant mortality, and fourth in maternal mortality among nations with populations of one million or more. But the real reason Singapore's healthcare system deserves to be called the world's best is because Singapore is the *only* nation in the top five in all three of these categories. Singapore is simply the best.

It's also consistent; Singapore proves itself to be the best overall performer year after year. In some years, Singapore comes in at number one in one or more of the individual categories as well. But even when Singapore doesn't top any of the individual categories, it still remains the overall champion. No other country can produce such excellent results so consistently across these three key healthcare metrics.

Now, you might object and say that three indicators are not enough to anoint any nation as having the world's best healthcare—and I'd agree with you, were it not for yet another piece of evidence. *Bloomberg Businessweek* magazine used twenty-one healthcare metrics when calculating its list of the world's healthiest countries in 2012. Those metrics included not only life expectancy at birth and infant mortality, but also death rates from communicable and non-communicable diseases, HIV infection rates, tobacco usage, obesity rates, environmental pollution rates, immunization rates, total cholesterol levels, alcohol consumption, and the degree of physical activity in which people engage.[2]

So what was Bloomberg's conclusion after including so many health metrics? As it turns out, Singapore has the world's healthiest people. Singapore is the world's healthiest country.

A look at the other countries on the Bloomberg list is also informative. Italy, Australia, Switzerland, and Japan round out the top five. Clearly, you don't have to be Asian or eat an Asian diet to make the top of the list. The pasta-loving Italians, beer-guzzling Aussies, and chocoholic Swiss do just fine without an Asian diet.

Hong Kong's rank (seventeenth) shows that you can't ascribe Singapore's excellence to being an extremely prosperous former British colony, or to being geographically small, or to Singapore having a mostly Asian population eating a mostly Asian diet, either. If those things made the difference, Hong Kong would be in second place behind Singapore, rather than in seventeenth place behind fourteen much larger, white-majority countries whose populations eat a Western diet. Also noteworthy is the fact that the two countries most often presented as models for US health reform—Canada and the United Kingdom—come in at fourteenth and twenty-first, respectively. Those are respectable ranks, out of the 145 countries ranked, but we should balk when presented with blandishments to copy the Canadian or UK healthcare systems. Why shouldn't we aspire to be like number one—Singapore— instead?

At the very least, nobody should model their healthcare system on that of the United States. Despite spending way more money per person on healthcare than any other nation, the United States ranks thirty-third on the *Bloomberg* list, coming in below much poorer nations like Greece, Portugal, Costa Rica, Chile, and Cuba—yes, the United States performs worse than Cuba, which spends just $830 per person per year on healthcare.

The question then becomes: How *does* Singapore deliver the world's best healthcare while simultaneously spending so much less than other countries?

The naive answer is: Efficiency!

The correct answer is: Incentives that *lead to* efficiency.

HOW IT HAPPENS

Let's first discuss efficiency, since we will spend most of the rest of the book talking about incentives for efficiency and how to set them up correctly.

Efficiency is the ability to get a lot of output from a little input. Table 3.2 demonstrates that Singapore is highly efficient when it comes to healthcare; it achieves spectacular healthcare outputs from truly modest amounts of inputs.

Table 3.2: Inputs of Physicians, Nurses & Midwives, and Hospital Beds, 2016

Country	Physicians per 1,000 people	Nurses and Midwives per 1,000 people	Hospital Beds per 1,000 people
Singapore	2.3	7.1	2.0
United States	2.6	9.5	2.8
Canada	2.6	9.8	2.6
United Kingdom	2.8	8.4	2.6
France	3.1	10.6	6.0
Japan	2.4	11.2	13.1
Sweden	4.3	11.9	2.3
Mexico	2.4	2.6	1.5
China	1.8	2.3	3.8
India	0.7	2.1	0.7
OECD Average	3.3	7.9	4.8

Sources: World Bank Health, Nutrition, and Population Statistics 2017, https://datacatalog.worldbank.org/dataset/health-nutrition-and-population-statistics; Occupational Outlook Handbook, Bureau of Labor Statistics, https://www.bls.gov; and OECD Data, https://data.oecd.org. The data for nurses and midwives is for 2016 except for the United States, which is for 2017. The data for hospital beds per capita and physicians per capita is for 2016.

Consider the first column of data, which gives the number of physicians per capita for each listed country as well as the average across all OECD countries. Singapore employs only 2.3 physicians per 1,000 people. The United States, by comparison, uses 2.6 physicians per 1,000 people—about 13 percent more than Singapore does.

If you scan down that first column in Table 3.2, you will see Singapore uses fewer physicians per capita than any of the rich countries—in fact, Singapore uses 30 percent fewer than the OECD average of 3.3 physicians per 1,000 people. Since it's also delivering the world's best healthcare, these small input numbers imply that Singapore is efficient; it gets more from less.

What's more, Singapore uses fewer nurses and midwives per capita than any other rich industrialized nation, as illustrated by the second column of Table 3.2. The OECD average of 7.9 nurses and midwives per 1,000 people is 11 percent greater than Singapore's 7.1 nurses and midwives per 1,000 people. The US figure of 9.5 nurses and midwives per 1,000 people is 34 percent greater than Singapore's figure. And the Japanese and Swedish figures are, respectively, 58 and 68 percent greater. Again, Singapore is doing more with less.[3]

The first two columns of numbers in Table 3.2, therefore, show that Singapore is efficient when it comes to human inputs (such as doctors, nurses, and midwives). The third column shows that Singapore is also efficient when it comes to physical inputs (like hospital wards, surgical suites, and rubber gloves).

The third column reports on the number of hospital beds per 1,000 people, a good summary measure of the volume of physical inputs used in a healthcare system. To understand why, you have to keep in mind that this statistic captures the overall amount of equipment and physical capital utilized by a healthcare system. Hospital beds are not bought in isolation. Each bed comes with a variety of associated equipment, including blood pressure gauges, heart rate monitors, and medical supplies. More beds require more rooms; more rooms require bigger hospitals, which end up with more MRI machines, larger surgical suites, and more TV sets to entertain patients. All this, of course, also comes with higher utility bills and larger maintenance costs. So the number of hospital beds per 1,000 people tells you not just about the number of beds, but also about the overall amount of physical capital that a healthcare system is using and must pay to maintain.

Taking all this into account, Singapore is shockingly efficient. It uses only two hospital beds per 1,000 people to deliver the world's best healthcare. By contrast, the US uses 2.8 hospital beds per 1,000 people, implying the United States needs 40 percent more hospital beds per capita to come in twenty-fifth in life expectancy, thirty-ninth in infant mortality, and forty-fifth in maternal mortality among countries with populations of at least 1 million people. If you count all the little countries too, then the US ranks forty-second in life expectancy, fifty-sixth in infant mortality, and forty-seventh in maternal mortality. When it comes to capital inputs as well as labor inputs, the United States does less with more. We are inefficient.

Let me take a moment to be nice to Iceland, though. Iceland spent only $4,116 per person on healthcare in 2015, or about $5,400 less per person than the United States. But it was still so much more efficient that it pummeled the United States in the rankings. All countries considered, Iceland came in at sixth in life expectancy, fourth in infant mortality, and fourth in maternal mortality.

Iceland's success further counters the idea that Singapore's success is only due to Asian genes, or an Asian diet, or being a small country. To begin with, the people of Iceland are predominantly blonde and white. They don't eat an Asian diet. Their success in healthcare costs and outcomes relative to the United States must therefore be chalked up to other factors.

Iceland and the world's other small countries also debunk the idea that Singapore's low costs and high efficiency can be attributed to its being small in either population size or geographic size. If a small population was what mattered, then the countries with fewer than one million residents should have lower costs than Singapore with its 5.4 million people—but they don't. And if a small geographic size was what mattered, then microstates like Monaco, Macau, and Lichtenstein that are truly tiny in geographic size should have lower costs than Singapore—but they don't.

LET'S BE BETTER

If we want to think seriously about designing a better healthcare system for the United States, we can't just fall back on ethnic or cultural stereotypes or blame it on our geographic size or large population. Those factors don't explain why both our outcomes and costs are so bad.

Our poor performance comes down to differences in healthcare institutions and incentives. Those differences explain how Singapore operates so much more efficiently, and they also give hope to all other countries. Good institutions and incentives are much easier to transfer from one country to another than are good genes, good diets, ideal geographic size, or ideal population numbers. Everything Singapore has done can be replicated. Why not give it a shot?

Chapter 4

America's Healthcare Humiliation in an International Perspective

I am not happy to be telling you about how wasteful and inefficient the US healthcare system is. I am American. My father was American. My mother, though Japanese by birth, was a physician here in the States. Born and raised in a little town in Japan, she was trained as an ophthalmologist and then practiced in the US. She even served as a medical officer for the US Navy after she became a citizen and completed her medical training.

I'd love to be able to brag not only about her talent as a surgeon but also about how my homeland delivers affordable, high-quality healthcare to all its citizens. But I can't because we have managed to create the world's least efficient healthcare system.

I presented statistical evidence for that in the last chapter, but allow me to share a visual. Consider Figure 4.1, which shows the percentage of GDP—national income—spent on healthcare in 2012

Figure 4.1: Healthcare Spending as a Percentage of GDP in the Thirty-Two High-Income OECD Nations, Plus Singapore, 2015

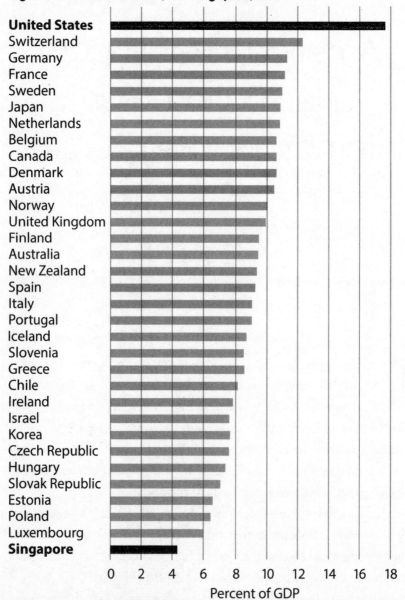

Sources: World Bank Health, Nutrition, and Population Statistics 2017, https://datacatalog.worldbank.org/dataset/health-nutrition-and-population-statistics; and OECD Data, https://data.oecd.org. There were thirty-four OECD countries in 2015. (Latvia joined in 2016 and Lithuania was added in 2018.) Two of the thirty-four were not high income: Mexico and Turkey.

for the thirty-four OECD countries, including the United States, plus Singapore (which is not a member of the OECD). In this figure, we can see how shockingly high US healthcare spending is, not only relative to Singapore, but relative *to all the other OECD countries* as well.

Americans love when Team USA finishes in first place at the Olympics. But when it comes to Figure 4.1, Americans should want to come in *last*, not first. It is an utter embarrassment that the United States is *first* in healthcare spending. Even more humiliating is that we also come in *way* higher on healthcare spending than even the second-place country, Switzerland. We spent 17.8 percent of our national income (GDP) on healthcare in 2015; Switzerland spent just 12.1 percent of its national income. We are the least efficient country when it comes to healthcare bang for the buck.

Consider once more those countries so often mooted as possible models for US healthcare reform:

- France registers 11.1 percent.
- Canada comes in at 10.4 percent.
- Sweden posts a figure of 11.0 percent.
- The United Kingdom punches the clock at 9.9 percent.

Meanwhile, Singapore quietly comes in last—the true winner of this race—spending just 4.2 percent of its GDP on the world's best healthcare. Even more impressively, Singapore spends substantially less than the next most frugal country, Luxembourg, which clocks in at 6 percent of GDP. Singapore isn't merely frugal; it delivers the best by spending the least.

Let me try to put this in perspective by comparing the nation of Singapore to Usain Bolt, the world's best sprinter. If we consider Singapore's super low healthcare spending of 4.2 percent of GDP to be equivalent to Mr. Bolt's world-record time of 9.58 seconds in the

100-meter dash, we can get a sense of just how far behind the other countries are in an event we might term the "Health Spending Sprint."

Luxembourg's 6 percent of GDP would be equivalent to running the 100-meter dash in 13.7 seconds. The United Kingdom's 9.9 percent of GDP would be the equivalent of 22.6 seconds. Canada's 10.4 percent of GDP would log in at 23.7 seconds. And France's 11.1 percent of GDP would equal 25.3 seconds.

The United States' 17.8 percent of GDP would be the equivalent of running the 100-meter dash in a pathetic 40.6 seconds. US healthcare spending is the equivalent of Usain Bolt running the 100-meter dash at top speed while Uncle Sam lightly jogs down the track. Bolt would finish thirty seconds sooner than Uncle Sam. To even call it a race would be a joke.

Sadly, US healthcare spending is just such a joke. We spend 75 percent more per person than Singapore but die 5.2 years earlier, endure an infant mortality rate more than 2.4 times greater, and have a maternal mortality rate that's nearly six times higher.

We need to learn how to run.

IT'S TIME TO CATCH UP

There have, of course, been many healthcare experts who have tried to teach us how to run. They usually point to Canada (23.7 seconds) or the United Kingdom (22.6 seconds) as models. But if we really want to learn how to run, I strongly believe that our best bet is to emulate the country that comes in first. That country is Singapore (9.58 seconds).

Our desperate need to pick up speed is further illustrated in Figure 4.2, which gives the dollar amounts spent per capita on healthcare in each of the thirty-two high-income OECD nations, plus Singapore, in 2015. (These values have been adjusted for international differences

Figure 4.2: Healthcare Spending per Capita in the Thirty-Two High-Income OECD Nations, Plus Singapore, 2015

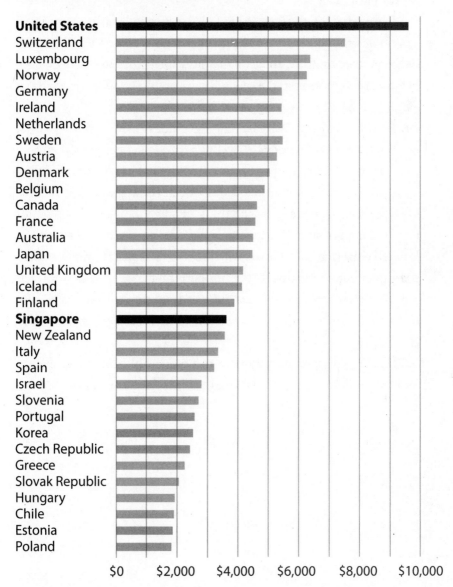

Sources: World Bank Health, Nutrition, and Population Statistics 2017, https://datacatalog.worldbank.org/dataset/health-nutrition-and-population-statistics; and OECD Data, https://data.oecd.org.

in price levels and purchasing power through the use of purchasing power parity calculations.)

Figure 4.2 shows that the United States spends far more per person on healthcare than any of the other high-income OECD nations or Singapore. In 2015, the United States spent $9,536 per person on healthcare. By contrast, the second-place country, Switzerland, spent $7,583, or $1,953 less per person on healthcare.

Figure 4.2 also shows that Singapore doesn't spend the *very least* per capita on healthcare; its 2015 figure of $3,681 per person is more than double the $1,704 per person spent by Poland, which spent the least per person on healthcare out of the thirty-two high-income OECD nations. So we shouldn't think of Singapore has having set for itself the goal of spending less on healthcare than any other country. If it had gone that route, it wouldn't be able to utilize the many expensive but effective treatments that modern medicine provides. Rather, *Singapore has figured out how to afford modern medicine's expensive but effective treatments while spending less per person than any other rich nation.*

If we're going to learn how to run our healthcare system better, let's run it like Singapore. Let's make it fast, efficient, and effective.

Chapter 5

What We Could Do If We Copied Singapore

What would the United States gain if we ran our healthcare system like Singapore's? Let's start with the potential benefits on which you *can't* place a dollar value:

1. If we could rise to Singapore's level of lifetime longevity, we could each, on average, enjoy another five years of sunsets, family gatherings, friendships, hobbies, travel, and community.
2. If we could drop to Singapore's level of infant mortality, we would cut the number of families that must mourn the passing of an infant by 59 percent.
3. If we could achieve Singapore's level of maternal mortality, we could cut the number of mothers who die while giving birth by 82 percent.

Matching Singapore's level of lifetime longevity alone would amount to an extra 1.65 billion years of life for Americans. That's quite a lot of sunsets and family gatherings and time spent with friends!

Now consider the benefits on which we *can* put a dollar value.

In 2015, the United States spent a little over $3.2 trillion on healthcare, which was 17.8 percent of that year's GDP of $18 trillion. Singapore spent only 4.2 percent of its GDP on healthcare that same year. With this information, we can put a precise dollar amount on how much we would be able to save if we, too, could run our healthcare system at only 4.2 percent of GDP. Multiplying 4.2 percent by $18 trillion, we see that US healthcare expenditures would only total $756 billion if we could get our spending rate down to 4.2 percent of GDP. That rate of spending ($756 billion per year versus $3.2 trillion per year) implies an annual savings of about $2.4 trillion per year.

$2.4 trillion *per year* is a truly enormous amount of money. To understand just how massive, let's compare $2.4 trillion to some other really big numbers:

- In 2015, the entire US defense budget (including all overseas military operations) totaled only $596 billion; our potential healthcare savings constitutes more than four times what we spend on our military each year.
- The US budget deficit was $439 billion in 2015; our potential healthcare savings is enough to balance the federal budget many times over.
- Only six nations—the United States, China, Japan, Germany, the United Kingdom, and France—have GDPs exceeding $2.4 trillion; you could run some awfully large countries (like Russia, India, or Australia) with what we waste each year on healthcare.
- Alternatively, you could run 139 of the world's smaller countries, foreign protectorates, and quasi-nations

simultaneously for less than $2.4 trillion per year
(including Costa Rica, Bolivia, Jordan, Botswana,
Albania, Armenia, Congo, Haiti, the West Bank, Bhu-
tan, Nepal, Belize, Andorra, and Tokelau, as well as
our good friend, Iceland).[1]

Another way to see how much money is at stake is to make some
comparisons in terms of percentages of GDP (gross domestic product,
anther way of saying national income). The 17.8 percent of GDP that
the United States spends on healthcare is 13.6 percentage points
higher than the 4.2 percent of GDP that Singapore spends on healthcare. The magnitude of that "13.6 percent of GDP" becomes immediately apparent when you consider that, in 2015, US defense
spending constituted only 4 percent of GDP; Social Security expenditures constituted only 5 percent of GDP; and that year's federal
budget deficit constituted only 2.4 percent of GDP. Each of those
figures is dwarfed by the 13.6 percent of GDP that we could recoup
by switching to a Singapore-style healthcare system. We could pay
for the entire federal budget deficit and then still have nearly $1.96
trillion left over to spend on other things.

One spending priority ought to be Social Security. By switching
to the Singapore system, we could save Social Security and bring it
into long-run actuarial balance by increasing our annual contributions to the Social Security trust fund by just 1 percent of GDP each
year.[2] And we'd still have another 12.6 percent of GDP to spend on
other things.

Of course, with respect to the entire 13.6 percent that we could be
spending on other things, conservatives and progressives would have
different spending priorities. Conservatives might want to balance the
budget deficit, increase defense spending, and use the rest for massive
tax cuts. Progressives would likely hope to direct the money toward
better social services, more Head Start programs, and pay raises for

teachers, police officers, and first responders. But no matter your political persuasion, I'm sure you won't find it difficult to imagine desirable ways our government could spend an extra $2.6 trillion.

I, for one, would like to see that money used to restore a growing and vibrant economy that will lift up the ordinary individual. I would like to see it used to restore hope and security to the average American, the regular guy or gal who only finished high school, lives in a working-class neighborhood, and toils long hours at thankless tasks for wages that are barely enough to keep a family afloat in this era of deindustrialization and global competition. *I think we should let America's workers keep the savings.*

If we could cut our health spending, this will happen naturally, and the major driving force will be the dramatically decreased cost of health insurance. In our highly competitive labor markets, this would cause an increase in take-home pay, since smaller fractions of total compensation would flow to employer-sponsored health insurance premiums (thereby freeing up money for higher wages and salaries).

And if we were to incentivize plentiful contributions to health savings accounts, working-class Americans would see tens of thousands of dollars piling up in their health savings accounts, dollars that would be their personal property—a nest egg to protect them and their families from medical catastrophes. Average Americans have lacked that security for far too long. I propose to let individuals keep most or even all of the savings that would result from switching to a Singapore-style healthcare system.

Even if you don't agree with that suggestion, the broader point remains: there is a lot we could be doing with 13.6 percent of GDP. But we can't get our hands on that money until we figure out how to run like Singapore.

Where to begin? Let's start by looking at our own system and its awful incentives.

Chapter 6

Why Is the US Healthcare System Doing So Badly?

Now we must ask the critical question: what makes the US healthcare system so *wildly* inefficient?

The answer: third-party payments. Why? Because they generate poor incentives. With third-party payments, no one has a strong incentive to limit costs or to "Just Say No" to wasteful spending.

Who is the "third party"? Imagine you go to see your doctor. In the relationship between you and your doctor, you the patient are the *first party*, while the provider, your doctor, is the *second party*. But much (if not all) of the bill for the doctor's services will likely be covered by *third parties* (such as Medicaid, Medicare, or private health insurance) who are not directly involved with providing or receiving healthcare services. Under this arrangement, payments don't flow directly from consumers to producers, as they do when you hire a lawyer or mechanic, or shop at Walmart or Target. Instead, payments flow from third parties to second parties, for services provided by second parties to first parties.

In competitive economic systems that have only first and second parties, second parties are incentivized to care about the interests of first parties. Second parties are forced to care, because they are competing with other second parties. Walmart didn't become the world's biggest retailer by delivering lousy service at massively inflated prices. If it had gone that route, it would have quickly found itself bankrupt. Walmart knows that its customers are first-party payers who are spending their own money directly out of their own pockets. If they don't like Walmart's product mix and prices, they will take their business elsewhere.

By contrast, our healthcare system has gone the route of lousy service at massively inflated prices. Our money flows not from first parties to second parties, but *from third parties to second parties*. It flows from Medicare, Medicaid, and private insurance companies to doctors, nurses, chiropractors, urgent-care clinics, imaging centers, hospitals, optometrists, audiologists, respiratory therapists, long-term care facilities, lab facilities, rehab centers, and so on and so forth. But in all instances, the fact that payments flow from third parties to second parties reduces the second parties' incentive to deliver what the first parties desire: high quality at low cost.

THE FALSE PROMISE OF "FREE"

Our reliance on third-party payments encourages overspending by all three parties and dissuades first parties from comparison shopping. Let me give you a real-world example. Consider the Hoveround brand of motorized wheel chairs, designed for elderly persons with mobility issues. In one Hoveround advertisement on the company's website, the very first message to which potential customers are exposed is: *"9 out of 10 people got their Hoveround for little or nothing!"*[1] Why does that message come first? Because Hoveround knows which feature its potential customers will find most seductive—it's hard to resist "free." Indeed, the promise of "free" is so attractive that Hoveround mentions it even before the headline promoting what the product can actually do for you: "Get Your Life Back with Hoveround!"

The rest of the page repeats "free" over and over:

- a *free* DVD kit,
- a *free* mobility consultation,
- the promise of *free* in-home training and delivery, and, best of all,
- "With Medicare and private insurance, your Hoveround could cost you little to nothing!"

Please don't think these promises are just a bunch of advertising hyperbole. They are, in fact, true statements. Hoveround's scooters really are totally free (or very nearly totally free) to older people with mobility issues. But free to individuals does *not* mean free to society. As first parties, Hoveround customers may pay little or nothing—but that is only possible because some third party ends up footing the bill. In this case, that third party is the taxpayer.

FIRST-PARTY INCENTIVES

Our system of third-party payments creates poor incentives for each of the three parties involved in a Hoveround purchase. Let's start with the first parties. By making Hoverounds free to first parties, our system has removed their incentive to weigh costs and benefits. To see how this drives healthcare spending up, let's consider my father. He died in his sleep at home a few years ago. He was eighty-six, surrounded by family, and had lived a long and interesting life. He could have used a Hoveround before he died, but he would have only really needed it for about four weeks before his death. Yet if he'd applied, Hoveround would have sent over one of its machines and billed Medicare for its full cost. As a result, the taxpayer would have been hit with a bill for thousands of dollars for a machine which would have been used for only a few weeks.[2]

By contrast, when people spend their own money, they tend to be circumspect and cautious. Understanding his own rate of decline, my father never would have spent $2,500 of his own money to purchase an MPV5 (Hoveround's most popular model) or $3,900 of his own money to purchase Hoveround's Teknique HXD (which can handle up to 450 pounds). However, when people are bombarded with advertising for something "FREE," they are implicitly being told that they no longer need to weigh costs against benefits; in fact, costs and benefits become totally isolated from one another. The user gets all the benefits while the taxpayer (via Medicare) pays all the costs. Consequently, people buy more Hoverounds than they ever would if they were confronted with the true cost, rather than this illusion of "free."

You might push back a bit and wonder if the second or third parties might be able to keep a lid on costs and wasteful spending. After all, first-party healthcare consumers are not the only decision makers involved in the purchase of a Hoveround. A first party's request for the device is not sufficient; a second-party physician must prescribe it, and a third-party insurer has to approve the payment. If we could trust that either the doctor or the insurance company would weigh costs and benefits sensibly, we might rest assured that the right decision would usually be made—that is, our healthcare system would only order and pay for Hoverounds when the benefits outweighed the costs.

SECOND- AND THIRD-PARTY INCENTIVES

Since first parties aren't incentivized to weigh costs and benefits, then second and third parties must be, right? Unfortunately, second and third parties are not in a good position to correctly weigh costs and benefits. They are stymied by two problems: poor incentives and incomplete information.

Let's start with the first problem: poor incentives. When doctors (and other second parties) are confronted with requests for Hover-ounds, they are not properly incentivized to investigate whether patients have a true medical need for it. Physicians are under considerable pressure to see as many patients as possible, and investigating whether every patient's mobility issues are serious enough and/or long-term enough to warrant a Hoveround is a time-consuming project. So, as you might expect, doctors are incentivized to be push-overs when it comes to these sorts of requests.

But even if detailed mobility exams could be done quickly and at a low cost, the doctor still knows that if he or she denies the request, the patient will probably go to another physician to seek approval. If that were to happen, the doctor might lose the patient forever. Here too, the doctor is faced with a difficult situation: approval would cost nothing, but rejection might cost him dearly. Once more, we see how second parties have an incentive to be pushovers with these requests.

A similar situation occurs when doctors are incentivized to prescribe antibiotics. Patients come in with colds (caused by viruses), but they demand antibiotics (which only work on bacteria). Doctors tend to go along with these requests, because many patients are convinced that antibiotics will help their colds. It is easier for doctors to acquiesce than to deal with patients complaining to hospital administrators or the threat of baseless (but nonetheless costly) medical malpractice lawsuits.

Acquiescing to baseless requests for antibiotics is just one example of "defensive medicine," which, unfortunately, is very common on the part of physicians. One 2005 study published in the *Journal of the American Medical Association* (*JAMA*) found that 93 percent of doctors in specialties with high litigation risks admitted to practicing defensive medicine.[3] They ordered MRIs or CT scans when X-rays would have sufficed, ran massive blood panels when testing for just a few things would have done the job, and sent patients in for unnecessary biopsies and screening tests. And yes, many also admitted to prescribing antibiotics for viruses. In fact, defensive medicine is so common that a 2010 Gallup poll of physicians found that the doctors surveyed attributed 26 percent of overall healthcare costs in America to defensive medicine.[4]

The decision to engage in defensive medicine is, on the one hand, understandable; it might cost a physician dearly to upset a patient, but it will cost very little to dump all the unnecessary costs of useless treatments, procedures, and prescriptions onto a third party. Faced with incentives like these, it's no wonder that 93 percent of doctors admit to practicing defensive medicine.

So what about the incentives facing private insurance companies? You might think that they would have a huge and obvious financial incentive to boost profits by denying claims. But that perspective demonstrates short-term thinking. The truth is, health insurance companies make a profit of about 5 percent on whatever gross volume of medical billing they happen to process. If they want larger absolute profits, then they need to make sure that the gross volume of medical billing goes *up* year after year, which obviously won't happen if they ruthlessly deny claims. They are actually incentivized to put up a relatively mild fight (and deny *some* claims), but mostly to rely on their ability to boost premiums year after year. With rising premiums, they have a larger pool of money for paying claims, which, in turn, means they can handle a larger gross volume of medical billing. By following this strategy, they can make a 5 percent profit on an ever-larger pool of claims. So private insurance companies have little long-run incentive to control costs. Their goal is to increase profits, and too much short-term cost control would hurt their long-run profits.[5]

On the other hand, government insurers (such as Medicaid and Medicare) don't even have the short-term profit incentive to deny claims. Because Medicaid and Medicare are legal entitlements, they must always lean in favor of paying claims. Medicaid and Medicare do try to keep a lid on costs by repeatedly reducing their reimbursement rates (i.e., how much they pay second parties for any given procedure). But second parties are not potted plants. They don't just sit there when you change their environment; they adjust their behavior to the new circumstances. Thus, when Medicaid and Medicare attempt to hold down spending by cutting reimbursement rates for specific procedures, second parties react by billing Medicaid and Medicare for a larger number of procedures or for a different set of procedures. By doing so, providers can keep squeezing as much money out of Medicaid and Medicare as they did before the reimbursement rates were cut.

What can Medicare and Medicaid do in the face of this? Not much. Their position as third parties means that they don't have access to direct information about what a first party's medical situation is, much less how it should be treated. Unable to know what is really going on with patients, third-party insurers are forced to trust and hope that second-party medical providers are not aggressively scamming the system.

WHO'S IN THE KNOW?

This constraint brings us to the issue of information and who can access it. Good decisions are only possible with good information.

Unfortunately, the third-party payer system tends to entrust payment decisions to those with the *least* information. The two people who have the most information about a patient's actual condition are the first and second parties (i.e., the patient and his or her doctor), but the ultimate authority for payment approval and cost control lies with third parties. And who are the third parties? They're either big government bureaucracies (located far away) or big private insurance companies (also located far away). Neither has the resources or the reach to gather all the relevant facts about each patient's medical situation, especially in light of tight legal restrictions on patients' medical information. With not enough time or money to police for waste and fraud, third parties are forced by necessity to approve payments on unnecessary prescriptions, unneeded procedures, and $2,500 Hoverounds for people who may not need them or who are unlikely to live long enough to justify the expense.

Third parties do have claims adjustors and insurance investigators who go out into the field and check around a bit. And third parties also put up a fearsome façade by suing the heck out of those caught engaging in insurance fraud. But with over $2 trillion in claims to handle annually, Medicare, Medicaid, and private insurers are in no position to discover whether most claims are medically valid. Getting the necessary information would be too costly—and too time-consuming.

This information does, of course, exist. It resides with patients and their doctors. But neither group has much incentive to restrain spending in our third-party payer system. As a result, both first and second parties overspend, and third parties are forced to go along because they lack the information needed to determine when costs exceed benefits.

The net result? Waste and inefficiency on a massive scale.

Chapter 7

Provoking Profligacy with Low Out-of-Pocket Costs

As I pointed out in the last chapter, the massive inefficiency of the US healthcare system is the result of our reliance on third-party payments rather than first-party payments. It is interesting to note that the greater that reliance has become over time, the worse our system has performed.

Consider Figure 7.1, which presents the percentage of all healthcare spending in the United States that has been paid for, out of pocket, by first parties (i.e., patients) rather than third parties (such as Medicare, Medicaid, the Veteran's Administration, and private insurers).[1] The data runs from 1960 to 2017, and it shows that healthcare spending paid for by first parties has declined dramatically over the past two generations.

Figure 7.1: Out-of-Pocket Healthcare Spending in the United States, 1960–2017.

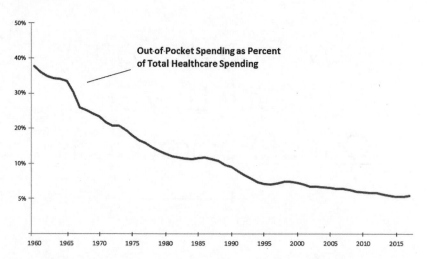

Source: OECD Health Data 2018, Organization for Economic Cooperation and Development (OECD).

In 1960, first parties in the United States paid *nearly 50 percent* of all medical spending directly out of pocket. By 2017, first parties paid for only about *11 percent* of all medical expenses directly out of pocket. Nearly 90 percent of all healthcare spending was covered by third parties that year.

The downward trend shown in Figure 7.1 has made healthcare seem increasingly inexpensive—in fact, almost "free"—to patients. But "free" has also generated increasingly poor incentives. The freer healthcare seems to first parties, the less they're inclined to weigh all costs against all benefits when making healthcare spending decisions. After all, why should they consider the impact of all costs when they only have to pay 11 percent of those costs? The other 89 percent is someone else's problem.

To get in that mindset yourself, take a moment to think about your favorite super-luxury car. Perhaps it's a Ferrari; maybe it's a Rolls-Royce. Think about seeing it parked in front of your house.

Imagine the sound of the engine, the smell of its hand-tooled leather, and how very comfortable and luxurious it is.

Now, consider whether you will ever purchase one.

Sadly, the fact that such cars typically cost $300,000 (or more) means that hardly any of us will ever buy one. Given our limited incomes, other things—like college for the kids and paying off the mortgage—will take precedence. That's reality. That's weighing all costs against all benefits and appreciating everything that we would have to forgo if we were to spend $300,000 on a luxury car rather than on more practical things, like college for the kids.

But what if I told you that you could be relieved from reality?

What if I told you that a third party was going to pick up 90 percent of the price of a Ferrari or a Rolls Royce and that you would only have to pay 10 percent of the total price? Instead of costing you $300,000, your dream car would cost you only $30,000. Since a 90 percent subsidy on a $300,000 Ferrari would make it even less expensive than the average Honda or Ford, demand would skyrocket. You and I—and most of the population—would rush to buy super-subsidized super-luxury cars.

Supply would also skyrocket. That is true because manufacturers wouldn't care how the total $300,000 price is split between the first parties benefiting from the subsidy and the entities providing the subsidy. As long as the manufacturers get their $300,000, they will gladly produce as many super-luxury vehicles as consumers demand.

Unfortunately, our healthcare system has gone down the same path, with third-party payers picking up the tab for nearly 90 percent of all healthcare spending. With everything from X-rays to Hover-ounds looking like they're 90 percent off, first parties have naturally demanded (and gotten) much more than they would have if they'd been confronted with unsubsidized prices.

The full folly of the first parties' overconsumption becomes obvious when you consider that a Honda or a Ford can do nearly everything that a Ferrari or Rolls-Royce can do—getting groceries, driving to work, or taking the kids to soccer practice. The only thing a Ferrari or Rolls-Royce is better at doing is conveying social status. So, inducing first parties to demand a Ferrari when a Ford would have been sufficient is pure waste.

But we haven't just subsidized wasteful healthcare choices over the past few decades; we've subsidized them more and more intensely, as indicated by the declining out-of-pocket spending shown in Figure 7.1. As the amount that people have had to pay out of pocket has declined, healthcare spending has gone way up.

So I drew the obvious conclusion: the massive increase in US health-care spending over the past two generations was caused primarily by the steep decline in out-of-pocket costs. But how confident can we be about drawing that conclusion? Could other factors have been more important (or at least significant) in driving up US healthcare spending? Were declining out-of-pocket costs *really* the primary factor driving the explosion in US healthcare spending?

It would, of course, be foolish to ascribe every little bit of the increase in US healthcare spending entirely to the decrease in out-of-pocket spending. But other potential culprits have not changed by nearly enough over time to explain the colossal increase in healthcare spending seen in the United States since the 1960s.

As just one example, consider supplier-induced demand—the tendency of doctors to overprescribe procedures when they will person-ally get a cut of the revenue. This happens, for example, with doctors who own their own X-ray machines. They are much more likely to recommend X-rays than doctors who send patients out to independent radiology labs to get X-rays. The tendency of supplier-induced demand to increase healthcare spending is well documented. But there is no evidence that supplier-induced demand has increased in intensity or frequency over time, which means it cannot plausibly explain the *massive* increase in healthcare spending over the past two generations.

The same is true of factors like expensive new technologies and medical malpractice costs. These do affect healthcare costs, but they haven't varied in intensity or frequency by nearly enough to explain the massive increases in US healthcare spending that we have seen in recent decades. The only factor that *has* varied enough to cause such an increase is the out-of-pocket spending ratio. As it decreased from nearly 50 cents on the dollar to just 11 cents on the dollar, the demand for (and supply of) healthcare services surged.

THE US AND THE REST OF THE WORLD

Yet another reason to believe that falling out-of-pocket costs have been the primary factor behind the massive increase in US healthcare spending comes from looking at US healthcare spending over time in comparison to the healthcare spending of other nations. Figure 7.2 displays the percent of GDP spent on healthcare by each of the OECD nations from 1970 to 2017.

Figure 7.2: Total Expenditures on Healthcare as a Percentage of GDP, OECD Countries, 1970–2017.

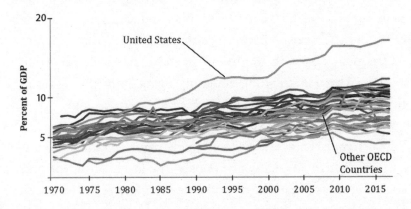

Source: OECD Health Data 2018, Organization for Economic Cooperation and Development (OECD).

See the line that pulls up and away from all the other lines as it extends toward the right side of the figure? That's the United States.

We clearly have a spending problem.

Sure, other countries also show a rising trend, but they've all managed to keep healthcare spending at about 12 percent or less of their respective GDPs. Only the United States has ever gone higher than 12 percent—and we did so way back in the early '90s.

Now look to the left side of Figure 7.2. You'll see the United States was among the highest spenders in 1970 (at a little more than 6 percent of GDP); but we were still *somewhat* comparable to the other OECD nations back then. Since around 1980, however, we've relentlessly pulled higher and higher.

Something must have been going on here that wasn't going on in the other countries.

WHY WE SPEND SO MUCH

We've been spending more and more than other countries since the '80s. Why?

It can't be because of expensive new medical technologies; it is no more expensive to build an MRI machine in the United States than in France. It also can't be supplier-induced demand or medical malpractice costs, because neither of these varied in intensity or frequency enough in any of the countries over this time to explain why our spending ended up being so much higher than that of any other OECD nation. Neither can we blame different levels of out-of-pocket spending across the various nations; most OECD nations had variations of "single-payer" national healthcare systems, which shared continuously low levels of out-of-pocket spending throughout the period shown in Figure 7.2. Since their out-of-pocket spending rates were static, those rates couldn't have had anything to do with the divergence of the United States seen in Figure 7.2.

The *only factor* that changed by enough to explain the divergence was the massive decline in out-of-pocket costs that occurred only in the United States. Those costs fell from around 35 percent of US healthcare spending in 1970 to just 11 percent in 2017, as more and more healthcare spending was paid for by third parties in the United States.

As third-party payments became overwhelmingly dominant, there was less and less incentive for first and second parties to limit spending. More and more spending decisions had to be made by third parties that had neither the incentive nor the information to make good decisions. As a result, US healthcare spending grew uncontrollably beyond both reason and benefit, as emphasized by Figure 7.3, which uses two vertical axes and two colors to display the long-run decline in out-of-pocket spending (black line and black axis) and the long-run increase in the percentage of US GDP that is spent on healthcare each year (grey line and grey axis). Between 1960 and 2016, while the out-of-pocket spending percentage fell from nearly 50 percent to only 11 percent, the percentage of US GDP devoted to healthcare rose from just 5 percent to nearly 18 percent.

Figure 7.3: Total U.S. Healthcare Spending as a Percentage of GDP and the Percentage of Total U.S. Healthcare Spending that was Paid for Out-of-Pocket, 1960–2016.

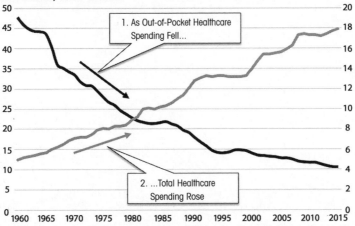

Source: OECD Health Data 2018, Organization for Economic Cooperation and Development (OECD) and National Health Expenditure Accounts 2016, Centers for Medicare and Medicaid Services.

So when you see that US line pulling away from all the other lines in Figure 7.2, it's because we've distorted our prices far more than any other developed nation.[2] This, in turn, has warped our incentives. We have unintentionally created the world's most costly and inefficient healthcare system. We must look for alternatives—in particular, alternatives that can handle the massive surge in demand that comes with low out-of-pocket costs. But before showing you the healthcare policies that are *actually* the very best in the world at solving those problems, let me in the next chapter discuss the single-payer systems that are often mistakenly *believed* to be the best solutions. They do indeed have mechanisms for dealing with low out-of-pocket costs and other problems, but those mechanisms fail on several counts—including delivering the world's best quality and lowest costs.

Chapter 8

How "Single-Payer" Systems Spend Less Than We Do

Now, at this moment, a small but plaintive doubt should come upon you. It will whisper softly: If low out-of-pocket costs are what's driving our healthcare spending out of control, how are nations like the United Kingdom spending less than we are on healthcare? After all, the United Kingdom, Canada, and other countries with national healthcare systems provide totally free care—that is, they have systems in which the out-of-pocket costs are zero. So why isn't spending getting even more out of control in those countries than it is here in the United States, where people are at least paying 11 percent out of pocket?

It's a good question. The answer is that centrally planned, single-payer healthcare systems use alternative methods to ruthlessly suppress the high demand caused by zero out-of-pocket costs. Consider the United Kingdom's National Health Service. It has an even bigger problem with low out-of-pocket costs than we do, because its guarantee to provide "free care" results in massively high demand for healthcare services. To deal with that massive demand, the National Health Service has implemented a large number of rationing mechanisms that rely on central planning to hold down both the total volume of expenditures as well as the total volume of treatment provided.

To see how these rationing mechanisms work, let's begin by considering the alternative situation, in which prices determined in *competitive* markets act as the rationing mechanism for scarce products, such as healthcare. Whenever you have a competitive market (where many buyers haggle simultaneously with many sellers), a single market price is quickly reached. That becomes the price at which anyone who wants to buy can buy and anyone who wants to sell can sell.

When all of those voluntary transactions are made between willing buyers and willing sellers, you will find that the quantity demanded by buyers at the market price will exactly equal the quantity offered by sellers at the market price. The total amount offered by sellers at that price will consequently flow only to those buyers who are willing and able to pay the market price. Only *those* buyers will get the amount that suppliers are willing to sell at that price. All the other buyers will get nothing. It is in that way that the limited supply offered by the sellers at the market price gets rationed, or allocated, among the buyers who showed up to the market on that day. Consequently, price mechanisms are a form of rationing—they allocate the overall quantity supplied to some buyers, but not to others.

When you offer universal free care (as the National Health Service does), you destroy any hope of using market prices as a rationing mechanism, because you intentionally don't run a market and don't allow prices to come into the picture. The problem with this strategy is that, whether you run a market or not, your offer of free care implicitly sets the price of healthcare at *zero*. At that price, people demand *a lot* of healthcare, because they are only confronted with potential benefits, while being completely shielded from any costs.

Thus, when you get rid of the price-rationing mechanism of markets you create the need for other rationing mechanisms besides price—non-market methods of allocating the limited supply of healthcare among all of the people demanding large amounts of healthcare at zero prices. During the 2008 US presidential contest, Republican vice-presidential candidate Sarah Palin caused a great deal of controversy when she asserted that countries with single-payer health systems use "death panels" to ration care. While her rhetoric may have been incendiary, it was essentially accurate. Any healthcare system offering universal coverage to all comers at zero price must have non-price rationing mechanisms to control costs. As it turns out, those mechanisms often look like panels of experts deciding who lives and who dies based on a cost-benefit analysis.

In the United Kingdom, the most powerful such body is the National Institute for Clinical Excellence (otherwise known as the NICE committee). This group of doctors, accountants, public health experts, and economists has a very sober task; they must set guidelines for how much the National Health Service is willing to pay to treat people. To set the guidelines, they basically ask the following question about any procedure that a patient might be demanding:

How much will this cost per additional year of life extension?

For example, suppose a patient is requesting an open-heart surgery that would cost £40,000. His doctor assesses his situation and determines that the surgery would extend his life by two years. Then, by dividing £40,000 by two years, the doctor determines that giving this patient an open-heart surgery would cost £20,000 per year of additional life. This is a crucial number because under the current NICE guidelines, the National Health Service will lean heavily toward approving any treatment that costs £20,000 or less per year of life extension. For treatments that cost between £20,000 and £30,000 per year of life extension, approval is possible, but only if

NICE can be convinced that the request meets some additional, hard-to-prove criteria (such as the "degree of certainty" that doctors have regarding their estimate of the probable number of years of life extension). Requests for treatments costing more than £30,000 per year of life extension are almost certainly going to be denied.[1]

To really understand what this means, imagine you are a parent. You have a little boy of, say, five or six years of age. He was a joyful ball of energy until he got sick. The best specialist in the country just informed you that he needs a rare and highly costly medicine in order to live. But rules are rules. If it costs more than £30,000 per year to extend your little boy's life, the National Health Service will refuse to pay, justifying their decision by saying that that money could be put to better use extending other peoples' lives for a longer amount of time. At that point, it's up to you to scrape together the money. If you can't, your little boy will die.

Once you understand that reality, Sarah Palin's rhetoric about "death panels" no longer seems so outrageous. When a government offers universal free healthcare to all comers, it has to create some sort of institution that can say *"No!"* and thereby ration the system's limited resources among all the competing healthcare needs of the entire population. But for those who are denied care, the NICE committee doesn't seem very nice at all. It looks and feels exactly like a death panel, deciding who lives and who dies by ruthlessly weighing costs and benefits.

OTHER NOT-SO-NICE WAYS TO RATION

The UK's National Health Service employs several additional methods for rationing its limited resources. Consider the ways in which it deals with the massive excess demand for specialist consultations that results from their having a price of zero. To begin with, the

NHS pays bonuses to general practitioners for keeping their referral rates low. This reduces spending because the only way NHS patients can see a specialist is if they can get a general practitioner to write a referral. No referral, no specialist.

The second method for squashing the demand for specialty consultations is to put the patients who do manage to get referrals onto long waiting lists (queues). This reduces demand in several ways. First, some patients don't even bother signing up when they see how long the wait times are. Others sign up but then get discouraged and drop off the list as time passes. And yet others die of old age or other infirmities before their names get to the top of the list.

The National Health Service also limits capital expenditures and restricts the supply of hospital beds and specialized equipment. If doctors have fewer hospital beds, X-ray machines, and brain scanners to work with, then that's another excuse for seeing fewer patients. Those capacity limits also create queues, which dissuade many people from seeking service in the first place.

The United States lacks a NICE committee. We have no centrally planned constraints on capital spending, no government-imposed limits on specialist referrals, and no spending limits based on the cost of an additional year of life extension. In our system, there is no institution that can say *"No!"* to the high levels of demand caused by low out-of-pocket costs. As a result, we end up spending much more on healthcare than the United Kingdom and other countries that use non-price rationing mechanisms to limit healthcare usage.

WHAT ABOUT INSURANCE?

In the United States, private health insurance is regulated mostly at the state level by insurance commissioners. In some states, these insurance commissioners are directly elected, while in others, they

are appointed by the governor. In either case, insurance commissioners are politicians, and they are subject to unrelenting lobbying by
special interest groups. Unfortunately, the desires of these groups are
often very expensive. Most groups lobby for insurance mandates—
that is, they lobby to get the state's insurance-coverage laws changed
so that every private insurance policy in the state will have to cover
whatever it is they provide.

The list of special interest groups includes homeopathic doctors,
hearing aid manufacturers, chiropractors, massage therapists, group
therapy counselors, acupuncturists, optometrists, pharmaceutical
companies, and medical device manufacturers, such as Hoveround.

Each special interest group lobbies for mandatory insurance coverage for *their* services, because they know that once insurance coverage becomes mandatory, the demand for their services will increase
dramatically. Workers will only be confronted with copays and
deductibles, rather than the full price of their services.

Naturally, *somebody* will have to pay for all that extra consumption. So insurance premiums will have to go up. But workers are
shielded from those costs because they think of their employers as
being the ones that have to bear the higher health insurance premiums. This, of course, is silly—firms just pass along those higher costs
by reducing take-home pay or withholding raises to make up for the
higher insurance premiums. Competitive firms only have a limited
amount of money available for total compensation (i.e., take-home
pay plus benefits). If more compensation has to be directed toward
paying for higher health insurance premiums, then less is available
for take-home pay.

Sadly, this trade-off is not widely understood. Many workers
think they should support insurance mandates in order to get something for nothing. Worse yet, their misunderstanding is self-reinforcing. High healthcare costs increase support for additional mandates,

but additional mandates lead to even higher healthcare costs. The process feeds upon itself, with nobody able to see that unsubsidized prices and real competition could deliver far better healthcare outcomes at far lower prices than our current process of adding more and more insurance mandates.

The full extent of this misunderstanding can be understood by comparing the costs of various elective and non-elective procedures over time. As the next chapter explains, the only medical procedures currently yielding both quality improvements and major price declines are the ones *not* covered by insurance.

Chapter 9

Empowering Prudence with First-Party Payments

The best way to demonstrate how third-party insurance payments drive up the cost of healthcare is by looking back at historical data. In particular, we can compare how the cost of medical procedures that *are* covered by health insurance have evolved over time relative to the cost of medical procedures that are *not* covered by health insurance.

Consider elective cosmetic surgeries, such as face lifts, nose jobs, and tummy tucks. Because insurance doesn't cover these procedures, people must pay for them entirely out of pocket. And thus, we get to see what happens to medical prices when insurance and third-party payments aren't involved.

What happens is that a vibrant and highly competitive market develops for these procedures. Because cosmetic surgery is paid for by first parties, first parties (i.e. patients) shop around for the best deals and take the time to research the doctors whose services they are interested in. Any doctor who gets a reputation for either low quality or high prices will lose customers. In order to thrive, a doctor must constantly innovate, stay one step ahead of the competition, and figure out how to consistently deliver outstanding outcomes at palatable prices.

To see the great effect first-party payments and competition have had on this slice of the healthcare industry, take a look at the four different inflation lines in Figure 9.1.

Figure 9.1: Overall (CPI) Inflation Compared with Medical Care Inflation, Physician Services Inflation, and Cosmetic Services Inflation, 1992 to 2013.

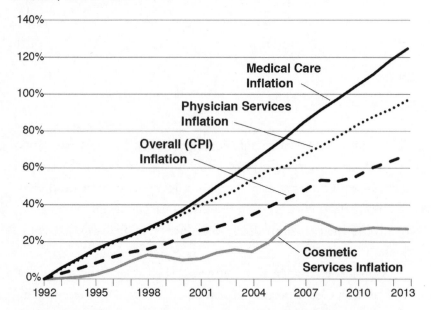

Source: "The Market for Medical Care Should Work Like Cosmetic Surgery," Devon M. Herrick, National Center of Policy Analysis, Policy Report No. 349 for 1992 through 2012, plus additional data from Devon M. Herrick to extend this figure through 2013.

Notes: Underlying data from the American Society of Plastic Surgeons and the Consumer Price Index (CPI), U.S. Bureau of Labor Statistics.

Let's start with the thick dashed line, which captures the overall amount of inflation (as measured by the Consumer Price Index) seen in the US economy across all consumer goods from 1992 to 2013. That line indicates that the overall level of prices in the economy rose by 67 percent during those twenty-one years. Over those two decades, however, medical care prices overall went up 125 percent (solid black line), while the prices paid for physician services went up 97 percent (dotted line). A comparison of these lines indicates quite starkly that healthcare prices rose much more quickly than consumer prices between 1992 and 2013.

By contrast, the real (inflation-adjusted) price of cosmetic services fell significantly during that time, as can be seen by the grey line. While the overall price level rose 67 percent, cosmetic services prices only went up by 27 percent. If you do the math, you will see that the real price of cosmetic services fell 24 percent over those twenty-one years.[1] By contrast, similar calculations show that the real, inflation-adjusted price of all medical care as a whole went up 35 percent over that same time period.

The fact that the prices for cosmetic services fell by 24 percent in real terms, while the overall cost of medical care in real terms rose by 35 percent, is by itself startling. But even more surprising is that the quality of cosmetic services increased dramatically during those twenty-one years. The techniques in use by the end of those twenty-one years were less invasive, required less time in the hospital, and involved much shorter recovery times at home. They even looked better. For evidence, just compare a celebrity nose job circa 1992 (Michael Jackson, for example) with almost any nose job done today.

Improvements in quality coupled with decreases in price also occurred in the field of eye surgeries designed to correct myopia, or nearsightedness. In 1992, the standard surgery for nearsightedness was radial keratotomy. This procedure involved taking a blade and making several radial cuts on the surface of the eyeball. As the cuts healed, they would tighten up, thereby reshaping the eyeball to correct the myopia.

The procedure could be very effective, but it required extremely skilled surgeons, and it was hard to predict how the cuts would heal or how much they would adjust the shape of the eyeball. Consequently, results varied, with only about half of all radial keratotomy surgeries resulting in perfect 20/20 vision.[2] Radial keratotomy also inconvenienced many patients, because surgeons would operate on one eyeball first and then, for safety reasons, wait six weeks before doing the other. Recovery took several weeks for each eyeball, and patients needed somebody else to drive them home after each separate surgery.

That being said, radial keratotomy was, at that time, the only game in town if you wanted to surgically fix your myopia. So it's not surprising that radial keratotomy surgeons were able to charge about $4,000 per eyeball in 1992—or about $6,692 per eyeball in 2015 dollars.

In 1999, the Food and Drug Administration approved an alternative to radial keratotomy. It was a laser-based myopia surgery called LASIK (laser-assisted in-situ keratomileusis). LASIK was wonderful; it simultaneously increased quality and reduced prices. In terms of quality, surgeons could perform LASIK on both eyes on the same day and the procedure had a substantially higher rate of getting patients to 20/20 vision. And the recovery process was so much shorter and easier that fully 92 percent of patients could drive themselves home, without glasses, immediately after the surgery.

In terms of prices, the original version of LASIK only cost $2,100 per eye when it debuted—substantially less than what radial keratotomy cost at the time. The cost savings then increased over time as the procedure became commonplace; competition arose among providers, and better types of LASIK were developed. By 2013, the original type of LASIK surgery cost only $1,543 per eye—a decline of 26 percent in nominal terms.[3] That by itself is impressive, but if you adjust for inflation, you will find that the real (inflation-adjusted) price of that original type of LASIK plummeted by a full 47 percent between 1999 and 2013.

Today, however, most people opt for an improved version of LASIK known as Custom Wavefront. Custom Wavefront made its debut in 2002. It literally takes ten minutes, and it produces higher-quality outcomes because it is entirely computer controlled and precisely tailored to the "fingerprint" of each individual eyeball.

Custom Wavefront is the current state-of-the-art procedure when it comes to LASIK surgery, but the original type of LASIK surgery discussed above was no less state-of-the-art when it debuted in 1999. An interesting price comparison can be made by comparing how much it cost at both points in time to obtain what was then the best possible LASIK surgery. In 1999, the best LASIK surgery cost $2,100 per eye, as noted above. By comparison, Custom Wavefront cost $2,177 per eyeball in 2013. So the price for state-of-the-art LASIK surgery went up by only seventy-seven nominal dollars between 1999 and 2013. Adjusted for inflation, that represents a 26 percent decline in the real cost of surgical myopia correction using each year's best LASIK technique. But because Custom Wavefront also represents a large increase in quality, the quality-adjusted gains have been even larger.

Looking back even further, it is also instructive to compare the 1992 price of radial keratotomy with the 2013 price of Custom Wavefront. In nominal terms, radial keratotomy on one eye would have cost you $4,000 in 1992, and Custom Wavefront for one eye cost $2,177 in 2013. That by itself amounts to a 46 percent decrease in the nominal price of myopia surgery. But if you adjust for inflation, you will discover that the real price of myopia correction decreased by nearly 70 percent over those twenty-one years, even while quality was massively increasing.

Looking back at Figure 9.1, you can see a similarly huge difference in the trajectories of inflation-adjusted prices over time when you compare cosmetic services (for which there are only first-party payments) and the overall cost of medical care and physicians services (where third-party payments dominate). Procedures paid for by first parties show strongly declining real prices over time, while procedures paid for by third parties show rapidly rising real prices over time.

THE LESSON TO BE LEARNED

Those massively divergent price trajectories are the result of three self-reinforcing factors:

1. Consumers demonstrate both prudence and frugality when they have to spend their own money; they carefully measure costs against benefits as they shop around for the best deal.
2. Anyone producing a healthcare product paid for by first parties must compete on both price and quality; that unending competition engenders continual improvements in quality and constant downward pressure on prices.
3. Intense competition also engenders aggressive advertising campaigns that inform potential customers about services offered and prices charged. Thus, useful information gets pushed out to potential patients, who otherwise would have never learned about all the available options.

Those three price-reducing factors are absent when third parties are paying. The result? Sky-high prices, no weighing of costs against benefits, and no competitive pressure to improve.

But before moving on, I'd like to dispel a closely related myth— the idea that expensive new technologies are driving up the cost of healthcare.

We can dispose of that myth by looking at Singapore and other rich nations. Expensive new technologies like linear accelerators, PET scanners, and 3-D image-guided stereotactic surgery robots are available in those other countries, too. Yet Singapore manages to deliver much better healthcare outcomes while spending 75 percent less than we do. So the availability of expensive new technologies *cannot* be the cause of our exploding healthcare costs in the United States.

But why not? Why is the myth untrue? Why aren't pricey new technologies responsible for at least some of the high cost of American medicine? After all, the United States in 2013 had way more MRI machines per capita than any other OECD country—34.5 MRI scanners per million people as compared with only 8.8 MRI scanners per million people in Canada and just 6.8 MRI scanners per million people in the United Kingdom. Heck, even the number two country, Italy, had only 24.6 MRI machines per million people, or nearly a third fewer per capita than the United States.

The United States clearly has a thing for expensive medical equipment. Thus, it is natural to suppose that our heavy use of expensive medical technologies is helping to drive our extremely high medical spending.

The problem with that story is that it gets cause and effect *backward*. Our use of expensive new technologies isn't the cause of our high healthcare spending; it's an effect. The underlying problem is a third-party payment system that incentivizes people to stop weighing costs against benefits. In particular, people begin to massively overuse costly new technologies when older, cheaper technologies would have worked just fine. Consider lower back pain. Unless there are neurological problems, the only type of medical imaging that is needed is an X-ray, which is very low-cost. But when a third party is picking up all or most of the costs, MRIs are often ordered because first parties lack any serious financial incentive to veto the more costly technology.

Hospitals, too, are complicit in the enormous amount of spending that flows toward expensive new technologies. For starters, expensive new equipment can be featured in advertising to help attract more patients ("We now have Gamma Knife surgery!"). Expensive new equipment also helps hospitals with recruiting, because most doctors love playing around with the newest and fanciest equipment. And because most of the costs will end up being paid for by third parties, hospitals don't have to worry too much about whether the costly new technologies really improve care enough to justify their hefty price tags.

Now compare that situation with the incentives that would follow if health insurance covered proven, time-tested treatments but not bleeding-edge new technologies. Because the patient would bear the full cost of opting for any costly new technology, she would weigh costs and benefits carefully and only opt for an expensive new treatment if its benefits clearly outweighed its costs. Singapore has created just such a system. Costly new treatments are available, but people are confronted with actual costs and real prices. This incentivizes people to make prudent decisions, both about their finances and their health.

Meanwhile, our system of third-party payments leaves us with inflated spending and low levels of efficiency. It incentivizes both first and second parties to overspend by blinding them to true medical costs.

Chapter 10

The Origins of America's Employment-Based Health Insurance System

You might wonder how we ended up with a third-party payer system that lacks strong incentives for anybody to say *"No!"* to out-of-control spending. The answer is that we accidentally constructed the only healthcare system in the world in which people think of health insurance as something they get from their employers. In no other country is health insurance coverage tied to employment or paid for primarily by employers.

Consider Germany. Germans are required to purchase health insurance, but German workers must help pay the premiums with their own money or, if they are poor, with money provided to them by the government. The insurance is also portable and not tied to any specific employer or even to being employed at all. If you end up unemployed in Germany, you will still have health insurance. Similar arrangements exist in France, Japan, South Korea, and several other rich industrialized countries. Both the United Kingdom and Canada have a national health service that provides care free of charge to all citizens by tapping general tax revenues. Only in the United States do we think of health insurance as something that is provided by employers.

One part of the Affordable Care Act of 2010 (also known as the ACA, or "Obamacare") tried to deemphasize the relationship between employment and insurance by creating a convenient marketplace where individuals could contract directly with insurance companies for health insurance. But the tradition of expecting insurance from our employers persists. As a result, Americans spend a lot of time worrying about their employer-provided health benefits, staying in jobs they hate because they're afraid to be without employer-provided health insurance, and delaying retirement until they're old enough to qualify for Medicare and be free of the need for employer-provided health insurance.

Things are also bad from the employer's perspective. The average cost of an individual health insurance policy was $6,896 in 2018, while the average cost of a family policy was $19,616.[1] Because people expect employers to pay most or all of the premiums for their policies, American businesses were traditionally faced with a substantial fixed cost for every employee they hired. That high fixed cost might have otherwise dissuaded firms from offering health insurance, but workers expected employers to give them health insurance. So firms were compelled to offer it.

Offering health insurance was often difficult for start-ups, small businesses, and even large corporations. Many business ventures that could have survived or thrived if they had *only* had to pay workers' wages were either pushed into bankruptcy or weren't even able to get started because of the additional burden of large insurance premiums.

The high cost of providing health insurance was also in large measure responsible for the rise of freelancers and independent contractors in the American economy. Firms could hire freelancers as outside consultants without having to buy them health insurance. That suited many young editors, programmers, and graphic designers quite well. Being unlikely to have major health expenses, they were fine with not having employer-provided health insurance. But the fact remains: they are without health insurance and will have no coverage if something does go catastrophically wrong.

How did we get here? How did we get into this mess?

America's dependence on employer-provided health insurance is a historical accident that has its roots in World War II price controls. During the war, most industrial production was redirected from consumer goods to war materiel. Ford, for instance, stopped producing civilian cars and trucks in order to devote all of its productive capacity to churning out 8,600 B-24 bombers as well as thousands of jeeps, M4 tanks, and supercharged V12 engines for British Lancaster and Mosquito bombers.

With little output flowing to the private sector, the government was worried about inflation. Inflation was likely because the economy had hit full employment, with Rosie the Riveter and her female compatriots helping to run factories twenty-four hours per day. All those workers were getting paid cash, so there was a lot of purchasing power floating around that could be directed at only a very small pool of civilian consumer goods (since so few civilian consumer goods were being produced). The natural result of any such situation of high demand and low supply is higher prices—that is, inflation. To forestall inflation and the negative effects that it would have had on civilian morale, the government fixed prices throughout the economy and simultaneously instituted a rationing program to allocate the limited quantities of civilian consumer goods to individuals.[2]

By fixing nearly all prices—including wages and salaries—the government had, however, created a problem for the industrialist

Henry J. Kaiser. Kaiser had made his first fortune paving roads in Cuba in the 1920s before becoming one of the largest contractors for the Hoover Dam, the Grand Coolee Dam, and the Bonneville Dam during the 1930s. Toward the end of the 1930s he established shipyards at several points along the West Coast and had a booming shipbuilding business thanks to low-cost mass production techniques, such as using welds instead of rivets.

When World War II began, Kaiser won the contract to produce thousands of Liberty ships, the sturdy cargo vessels that the US military would use to transport soldiers and weapons to both Europe and Asia. But with wages fixed by law, Kaiser initially had a hard time recruiting enough workers to his Pacific Coast shipyards. The West Coast was still very lightly populated at that time. The only place he could get enough workers was back East. In particular, Kaiser needed to get tens of thousands of people to move themselves and their families from places like Detroit, Michigan to places like Richmond, California and Vancouver, Washington.

Forbidden from offering higher wages as an inducement, Kaiser cleverly offered his employees free healthcare. This was a natural innovation for him, because he had previously hired a medical doctor to live out in the Nevada desert to take care of the workers who helped to build Hoover Dam. Offering free healthcare provided a way around war-time wage and price controls because health benefits were considered to be neither wages nor salaries. They were defined to be fringe benefits and thus free from wage and price controls.

By the end of the war, many major US corporations had joined Kaiser in giving employees free healthcare as a way of competing for scarce labor resources. When wage and price controls ended after the war, the unique US system of employer-sponsored health insurance was well established and continued out of habit during the boom years that followed.

A change in the tax laws in 1954 guaranteed that the system would remain in place indefinitely. The Internal Revenue Code was updated that year to include a permanent tax exemption for employer-sponsored health insurance. That exemption would guarantee that employees would thenceforth always prefer to get their health insurance coverage through their employers rather than buying it for themselves directly from insurance companies.

To see why, suppose that your employer is currently compensating you with both wages and health insurance. To be more specific, suppose that your employer is paying you an annual salary of $50,000 per year while also paying a $20,000 premium for a health insurance policy that covers you and your family. Adding together your salary plus the money that your employer is spending to cover your health insurance, your total compensation is $70,000.

If it weren't for the 1954 exemption, you would have to pay income taxes on all $70,000 of that total compensation. But thanks to the 1954 exemption, you do not have to pay any taxes on the $20,000 in healthcare benefits. (By contrast, other types of fringe benefits are taxable. So if your employer had given you a car worth $20,000 as a gift or awarded you a $20,000 shopping spree in Paris as a bonus, you would still have to pay income taxes on the $20,000 value of those items.)

To see why the tax exemption for health insurance implies that people would rather have their employers purchase their health insurance, suppose that your employer suddenly decides that he no longer wants to bother with providing health insurance. Instead of paying an insurance company $20,000 to cover you and your family, your employer tells you that, instead, he is going to give you the money. That is, you will get a $20,000 per year raise with which you can go out and buy your own health insurance coverage for yourself and your family.

The problem is that your $20,000 raise won't be tax exempt. It will be taxed at whatever marginal tax rate applies to your level of taxable income. For simplicity, let's assume that you and your spouse fall into the 20 percent tax bracket. At that rate, you would end up paying $4,000 (or 20 percent of $20,000) in taxes on the $20,000 raise. As a result, you would only have $16,000 left over out of the original $20,000 to spend on a health insurance policy for your family. So you would either have to settle for a less expensive policy that offers poorer coverage or figure out some way to rearrange the rest of your budget to come up with the $4,000 necessary to make up for the money you just lost in taxes. Unless you can come up with that $4,000, you will end up with worse health insurance coverage.

Once you understand this dynamic, it becomes clear why US employees will always strongly prefer to have health insurance paid for by their employers. That being said, the current system only feels natural because nearly all of us grew up after 1954. We don't remember the era before the tax exemption was put in place. We don't remember when individuals were much more in touch with costs and benefits because they paid for their own health insurance premiums.

But while the current system may feel perfectly natural due to its familiarity, we certainly don't have to perpetuate it. It is the result of a historical accident and the world has already figured out how to design better insurance systems—insurance systems that can incentivize people to weigh costs and benefits, avoid wasteful spending, and keep a lid on unnecessary expenditures.

Chapter 11

How to Engineer Low-Cost Health Insurance

Insurance is popular because it shields people from risk and uncertainty. At the same time, however, people should be vigilant about the fact that insurance payments are third-party payments—the kind of payments that lead to wasteful spending. We should investigate how to set up an insurance system so that the benefits that it provides in terms of protecting people from risk and uncertainty are not overwhelmed by the bad incentives that it creates via third-party payments.

But before I delve into the intricacies of different health insurance systems, let me first define some insurance terminology. Under a private insurance contract, an individual pays a fee—known as a *premium*—to an insurance company in order to obtain the right to receive monetary compensation if one or more pre-specified events comes to pass. In the case of fire insurance on a home, there's just one pre-specified event: a house fire. The monetary compensation in that case would be based on the dollar value of damaged household items as well as reconstruction costs. In the case of automobile insurance, the set of pre-specified events would typically include car accidents that cause either property damage or injury to one or more persons. In the case of health insurance, the set of pre-specified events is typically quite long—everything from annual checkups to radiation treatments to tonsillectomies to prescription drug coverage.

When a pre-specified event occurs, you can file a *claim* with the insurance company to have them pay out in whatever way is specified in the insurance contract. If the insurance company approves the claim and agrees that one of the pre-specified events occurred, it will typically pay an appropriate second party on your behalf—a construction guy to fix a home gutted by fire, a body shop to fix a bent fender, or a physician for an eye exam. In other cases, the insurance company will simply write you a check.

A key point is that the insurance contract can be modified in several ways to adjust how much of the total cost of a claim will be paid by the third party (the insurance company). This can be accomplished by modifying either the deductibles or the copays. A *deductible* is a monetary limit below which individuals holding insurance policies cannot file claims. For example, if John has a car insurance policy that has a $2,000 annual deductible, he cannot file any claims with his insurance company until the total cumulative cost of all the pre-specified events since the start of the current calendar year has totaled at least $2,000. If they total less—say, $1,300—then John will have to pay for them entirely out of his own pocket as a first-party payer.

It's crucial to note that, below the deductible, there are no third-party payments. First parties will pay everything—which implies that first parties will have a strong financial incentive to be careful comparison shoppers and seek out the least costly way to fix whatever damage has occured up to that point. Deductibles also cut down on paperwork and overhead for insurance companies, since no claims can be filed until cumulative spending reaches the amount of the deductible. Until that threshold is reached, paperwork is light.

Unfortunately, it is also possible to structure insurance policies so that they have zero deductibles, or what is commonly referred to as *first-dollar coverage*. Such contracts are highly problematic, because every pre-specified event becomes claimable and thus subject to third-party payments and all of the bad incentives associated with third-party payments.[1]

Copayments, or *copays*, are another way in which insurance contracts can be modified to adjust the fraction of total payments that will be made by the third party (the insurance company) rather than by the first party (the insured person). But before talking about copays, it is necessary to be clear about terminology; different English-speaking countries have different definitions for the word copay and for the closely related concept of coinsurance.

Let's examine the US definitions first. In the United States, the word copay refers to a fixed dollar amount that an insured person must pay to access a medical service before the insurance company will pick up the rest of the bill. An example would be a mandatory $15 charge for office visits. That value is always the same, irrespective of whether an office visit costs $50 or $500 or whether the insured person is going in for the first time or the fiftieth time.

Then there is coinsurance. In the US, coinsurance refers to a situation in which the insured person has to pay a fixed percentage of a bill (rather than a fixed dollar amount) before the insurance company will pay for the rest of a claim. The required percentage only applies to claims that are filed after the deductible is reached and is sometimes also capped on the upside at a certain maximum cumulative value. As an example, the individual's coinsurance rate might be 20 percent of all claims above a $2,000 deductible up until a

$10,000 annual limit is reached; after that limit is passed, 100 percent of all further claims will be paid for by the insurance company.

In contrast to the US habit of distinguishing between copays and coinsurance, Singaporeans use the word copay to encompass both concepts. But, because Singapore's health insurance system makes use of fixed percentage payments almost exclusively, the word copay in Singapore normally refers to what Americans would call coinsurance.

For the purposes of this book, I am going to go with the Singaporean terminology and simply refer to copayments and copays throughout this work, as I believe that the term copayment correctly captures what is actually going on (i.e., the first party and the third party are sharing the cost of a claim). The term coinsurance, by contrast, makes it sound as if the first and the third parties are somehow enrolling for insurance together as mutual first-parties—rather than one being the first party making claims and the other being the third party paying them out. Using the Singaporean terminology will also enable you and other readers of this book to acclimate to the Singaporean definition of the word copay. If you go on to read anything else about Singapore's healthcare system (such as the Singapore Ministry of Health's website), you will already understand that Singaporeans use the term *copay* to refer to the insured person having to pay a fixed percentage of any bill in excess of the annual deductible.

To see how Singaporean-style percentage copays work, think again of John, the guy with the car insurance policy that has a $2,000 annual deductible. But now imagine that he also has a 10 percent copay for any spending above the deductible. Also suppose that John is having a bad year. In February, he skids on ice, loses control of his car, and crashes into a tree. The repair costs $2,000, which he has to pay entirely out of his own pocket because he has not yet exceeded the annual deductible. Then, in July, he gets caught driving during a massive hailstorm. Three minutes of golf ball-sized hail causes $3,000 worth of damage. Since that damage is in excess of his annual deductible, he can file a claim. But because the policy requires a 10 percent copay, John would have to pay $300 of the $3,000 while the insurance company pays the other $2,700.

Note that the copay is a first-party payment. That matters a great deal if you want John and other first parties to have an incentive to shop around for the best deal. True, John's incentive to find a high-quality, low-cost repair shop is not nearly as great when he is paying a 10 percent copay as it would be if he were paying for the entire bill out of his own pocket. But $300 is still $300. So John will have at least some incentive to hold down costs.

Even better, the percentage nature of the Singapore-style copay means that any savings that John manages to dig up will be shared with the entire insurance system. If John can get the repair done for $2,000 rather than $3,000, it will not only be the case that his share will fall from $300 to $200; the insurance company's share will also fall, from $2,700 to $1,800. That is an important fact because the only way to lower insurance premiums over the long run is to reduce the amount of money that insurance companies have to pay out on claims. When copays motivate first parties to cut back on wasteful spending, insurance premiums can be lowered throughout the system.

As you might imagine, Singapore has utilized both deductibles and copays to mitigate the waste and inefficiency that result from third-party payments. Singapore has set both types of "cost sharing" at high enough values that for the vast majority of health care needs—routine checkups, immunizations, arthritis medications, etc.—people are either operating below their annual deductible or are confronted with a large enough copay to cause them to weigh costs and benefits wisely and shop around for the best deal.

Singapore also forces its residents to weigh costs and benefits by confronting them with the cost of their health insurance premiums.

This is easy to do because, unlike the United States, Singapore has no entrenched tradition of employers paying for their workers' health insurance. Individuals buy their own health insurance and are consequently confronted with its full cost.

By contrast, workers in the United States typically have no idea how much their employers are paying for their health insurance coverage. That makes health insurance seem free. But when health insurance seems free employees lack any incentive to consider different insurance offerings, including those that have lower premiums because they feature higher deductibles or only cover core medical services like annual checkups and hospitalizations. In addition, workers who are offered "free" health insurance tend to want first-dollar coverage and policies that cover anything and everything.

That is hugely problematic. Including more and more treatments without confronting people with costs promotes unnecessary treatments and overconsumption. Not only is it wasteful, it also drives up the price of health insurance premiums for everyone else. As an example, consider how much more expensive automobile insurance would become if it included car washes, oil changes, and unlimited gasoline rather than just collision and liability coverage. With car washes included, a lot of people would get their cars washed all the time. The same would be true with oil changes and definitely with gasoline. By including them in the insurance policy, you have incentivized people to consume a lot more than when they must pay for all of those items out of their own pockets.

This tendency for people to change their behavior when somebody else is picking up the tab is called "moral hazard". One of Singapore's primary goals is to set up financial incentives that will mitigate moral hazard. The purpose of deductibles and copays is to confront people with costs so that they have a financial incentive to avoid overconsumption and wasteful spending.[2]

Another way to understand Singapore's success with deductibles, copays, and making people pay for their own insurance premiums is by drawing an analogy between health insurance and what economists and political scientists like to call the "common-pool problem". The common-pool problem arises when a commonly held resource ends up being overused and destroyed because anyone can use it for free as much as he pleases. The ecologist Garrett Hardin brought the common-pool problem into popular discourse with his famous 1968 article in the journal *Science* entitled, "The Tragedy of the Commons." Hardin's paper gave as its primary historical example the publicly owned grazing pastures that many communities in England maintained during the Middle Ages. Those plots were referred to as commons because they were held in common (that is, publicly).

The commons were created as a social safety net. Each provided a few acres where the poor could graze animals and thereby provide meat and dairy products for their families. But, because they were commonly held, the plots were in fact open to all people equally. Anybody could graze his animals for free, without having to pay anyone else for the use of the land.

Unfortunately, that setup meant that the land became overused and totally stripped of grass—so that it wasn't of any benefit to anybody, rich or poor. The problem was that each person knew that there was both a limited amount of grass and nothing stopping anyone else from getting to it first. So everybody rushed to get as many animals as possible onto the commons plot each spring. The result was catastrophic overuse. In a matter of days, the grass was eaten down to the roots and the plot was trampled into a muddy mire.

Allowing unfettered common access to the plots was equivalent to privatizing benefits while socializing costs. Whoever got his animals onto the plot first got to keep the limited supply of benefits for himself. But the cost of the ruined land—and of the lost opportunity to help the poor—was shared by all.

Similarly, insurance can suffer from the same bad incentives when first-party payments are low or nonexistent. Insurance companies only have a limited amount of money to pay out on claims, because claims payments can never exceed the amount of money collected in premiums. That is similar to the commons plots only having a limited amount of grass-growing capacity. If you then present the insured with free or nearly free care, they are placed into a Tragedy of the Commons situation in which each person has an incentive to consume as much as possible as quickly as possible before anybody else does. There's only a limited pile of money for claims, and whoever files first will get the money.

To prevent that dynamic from overwhelming their healthcare systems, countries that offer unlimited free healthcare, such as the United Kingdom, have had to set up rationing mechanisms that prevent participants from racing to use as much of the limited healthcare budget as possible before anyone else does. The rationing mechanisms are the equivalent of putting a fence around a medieval commons plot and making up a bunch of rules that limit who has access to it. It's the only way to prevent the UK's single-payer system from being overwhelmed by consumers.

Singapore's solution is different. Instead of imposing rationing on people externally by queuing or denial-of-care thresholds (how NICE!), Singapore has enabled people to self-ration by confronting them with costs and prices. The benefits of healthcare are still there, but people are forced both to acknowledge and share the cost of providing those benefits. The result is much less waste, as people only consume the treatments for which the benefits they receive personally outweigh the costs they must pay personally.

The equivalent with respect to medieval commons plots would have been to charge a price to graze each animal. The price could have been quite modest, but any positive price would have made people think twice. And, if you'd set the price correctly, people would have put out only as many animals as the land could support.

So too with healthcare. Confronting consumers with prices forces them to face reality. Medical care is costly, and it is unfair to think of the healthcare system as a common resource from which you can take as much as you want without bearing any of the costs. To prevent that, Singapore has implemented a health insurance system in which people have to pay their own premiums and in which there are both substantial deductibles as well as substantial copays. By confronting consumers with the reality that care costs money, Singapore has short-circuited the bad incentives that led to the Tragedy of the Commons.

Meanwhile, we haven't. We lack the non-price rationing mechanisms used by the United Kingdom, and many of us are exempt from the sobering economic reality check imposed by substantial deductibles, meaningful copays, and having to pay one's own insurance premiums. We have designed a healthcare system with the same incentives that the Tragedy of the Commons had. It is no surprise, then, that people overuse and waste.

Our only response has been to throw more money at the system each year, as though the correct solution is to set up additional commons plots. By following that path, we have ended up spending nearly 20 percent of our national income to support a bunch of muddy, mediocre plots whose productivity is so low that we are ranked forty-second in life expectancy, fifty-sixth in infant mortality, and forty-seventh in maternal mortality.

By contrast, Singapore's plots are so productive that with an expenditure of less than 5 percent of GDP, its residents enjoy the world's best healthcare. The next few chapters explain how Singapore does it.

Chapter 12

Visiting Singapore's Hospitals and Clinics

Before delving into its policy details, let me walk you through Singapore's healthcare system at the ground level, the way you would experience it if you took a trip to Singapore and spent a few days poking around and asking questions. My description won't be as much fun as watching the movie *Crazy Rich Asians*, but you can think of this chapter as giving you a sneak peek at crazy cheap healthcare.

My first trip to Singapore was a one-man research junket. I went as a private citizen and simply visited hospitals and clinics on my own. I spoke privately with doctors, nurses, dentists, patients, former health ministry officials, hospital administrators, clinic directors, and every taxi driver, waiter, and shoeshine boy with whom I could strike up a conversation. I also had the good fortune to meet several health professionals socially through the Rotary Club of Tanglin. For a solid week, I investigated, interviewed, and questioned, putting to work everything I had learned as a high school journalism student (thank you, Mr. Graves!).

A year later, thanks to the dynamic and irrepressible Mei Lin Fung (who found a video of me discussing Singapore's healthcare system on YouTube), I got to be an unofficial guest of the government. I spent ten days meeting with community clinic directors, public and private hospital administrators, the heads of non-profits, government health economists, doctors, nurses, dentists, public health officials, and even the permanent secretary for health (the highest-ranking civil servant in the Ministry of Health).

WHAT I SAW

So here's what it's like in Singapore: There are both public and private hospitals, as well as public and private clinics. The public hospitals dominate acute medicine, delivering over 80 percent of Singapore's acute care (time-critical, short-term treatments for things like severe injuries, heart attacks, strokes, poisoning, and recovery from major surgery). On the other hand, private clinics deliver over 80 percent of Singapore's primary care (non-emergency walk-in appointments with general practitioners for things like annual checkups, sore throats, immunizations, dietary advice, and the management of chronic conditions like diabetes and hypertension).

The 20 percent of primary care provided by the public sector is delivered by eighteen neighborhood polyclinics. These polyclinics are one-stop shops for primary and preventive care. They deliver government-subsidized outpatient care, health screenings, and pharmacy services. Patients can stop by and get treated for everything from abdominal pain to zinc deficiencies. They can also get prescriptions filled at on-site pharmacies, have their eyes checked for glaucoma, enroll in an infant nutrition program, get examined when they take a fall or twist an ankle, and basically get treated for anything that doesn't require acute care, a specialist, or inpatient treatment. Nine of the polyclinics also offer dental services.

The polyclinics themselves are typically three- to four-story buildings. They are located in neighborhood centers and situated so that they are easily accessible by public transportation. At the entrance, there are greeters as well as medical social workers. The medical social workers act as ombudsmen and advisors, making sure that each person knows which government benefits he is eligible for and how to apply for them. After checking in, patients enjoy comfortable waiting areas for each type of care. Most patients will have arranged appointments ahead of time, but the polyclinics also take drop-ins for urgent care.

The polyclinics that I visited were clean, orderly, and modern. Most were either recently constructed or recently remodeled, even in working-class neighborhoods. Care is available at polyclinics for people of all income levels, but as I will explain over the next few chapters, the government has set things up so that any affluent person who uses a public hospital or polyclinic will pay substantially more for services than will those of lesser means.

FREEING HOSPITAL EMERGENCY ROOMS FROM HAVING TO PROVIDE PRIMARY AND URGENT CARE

Polyclinics were intentionally created to manage primary care (including urgent and preventive care) so that Singapore's hospitals could be freed up to handle acute care. By contrast, acute-care hospitals in the United States also have to deliver a large volume of primary-care services, especially in their emergency rooms.

My mother worked at Los Angeles County Hospital after completing her residency in ophthalmology. Los Angeles County Hospital is a large, government-funded, free-care facility in LA, and is run in conjunction with the University of Southern California's medical school. Its resources should be concentrated on acute care for the poor, but its emergency room becomes swamped every day by indigent patients who lack any other way of accessing primary healthcare services. The emergency room is so overcrowded that wait times have been known to exceed twenty-four hours.

By contrast, Singapore's well-designed and financially accessible polyclinics have solved those problems. If the impoverished need primary care, they can go to polyclinics. If they need acute care, they can go to hospitals. Because each type of facility can concentrate on its intended purpose, wait times are short and service quality is high.[1]

As I mentioned above, private clinics deliver 80 percent of Singapore's primary care. Some of these clinics look like American-style urgent care centers with multiple doctors, while others have just a single doctor working in private practice. Private clinics are in every neighborhood, practically on every block, which engenders friendly competition between Singapore's primary care physicians. They must deliver high-quality services at attractive prices if they are to keep their clients.

SINGAPORE'S TIERED HOSPITAL SYSTEM

Singapore's hospital system is organized into several tiers, with each tier specializing in a different set of medical services. *Acute general hospitals* are what Americans normally think of when they hear the word hospital. They are inpatient facilities set up to treat any sort of acute illness or severe trauma. They have emergency rooms and the facilities necessary to perform major surgeries. These hospitals handle things like open-heart surgery, neonatal care, severe burns, orthopedic surgery, motor vehicle trauma, and poisoning cases.

Of the sixteen acute general hospitals in Singapore, nine are private and seven are public. The public hospitals are much larger, however, with the largest, Singapore General, having 1,700 beds. By comparison, the largest private hospital in Singapore only has 345 beds. As a result, 85 percent of Singapore's acute-care hospital beds are in the public sector.

Specialty centers are similar to acute general hospitals except that they *only* deliver acute care within their respective specialties—cardiology, ophthalmology, oncology, neuroscience, dermatology, and dentistry. All six of these are public, and because of Singapore's small size, none are located very far from the large majority of the population.

The public sector also runs a women's and children's hospital, as well as a major psychiatric hospital. KK Women's and Children's Hospital provides specialty care to women in areas that include fertility treatments, breast cancer, maternal medicine, and menopause, and to children in areas that include children's cancer treatments, children's craniofacial surgeries, developmental endocrinology, and children's ophthalmology. The Institute of Mental Health specializes in inpatient psychiatric care designed to return individuals to normal functioning in the community.

VISITING SINGAPORE GENERAL

To give you a first-person perspective on Singapore's hospital system, let me tell you what it's like to visit Singapore General, the largest and oldest public hospital in the country.

I was shocked when I first visited "Sing Gen," because my idea of a large public hospital was Los Angeles County Hospital—overcrowded, run-down, and with a staff so continually overwhelmed that they are often unable to give patients enough time or attention.

By contrast, Singapore General manages to be friendly, clean, modern, and uncrowded, despite bustling with patients and visitors. It operates at about 85 percent capacity, as do Singapore's other public hospitals.

Even better, Sing Gen is staffed to maximize customer service. At each entrance, there is a covered carport, so that patients using cars or taxis can get in and out without ever having to worry about Singapore's torrential tropical downpours. You will find porters waiting to help people with their baggage, to help them in and out of vehicles, and to get them in and out of wheelchairs—in fact, they'll wheel you anywhere you need to go. The porters' services are totally free, and you're forbidden to tip them.

A few feet away, just inside the entrance, there is a meet-and-greet counter staffed by friendly hospital receptionists as well as medical social workers. The receptionists help patients figure out where they need to go, while the medical social workers are available to offer advice on various public subsidies, whether a patient qualifies for them, and how to obtain them if he does.

As soon as the patient checks in for his appointment, he is assigned a number, sort of like the numbers you take at certain fast-food restaurants in the United States to see who's next in line. But Singapore General isn't interested in who's next; it's interested in getting people where they need to go. To that end, there are large computer screens in each waiting room and then smaller ones above each examination room. The screens display patient numbers in a guiding way, so that, for example, the screen outside the Radiology Department displays the numbers of the patients who should be heading over to Radiology at that moment. And when they are done with their radiology appointments, those patients' numbers will be displayed, if necessary, outside whatever location each respective patient should be heading to next. It is like a trail of breadcrumbs leading the patient through the hospital. Even better, the patient's doctor can know with confidence that when he meets the patient, it will be the right patient. He only has to check the number.

Things are equally efficient in the emergency room—or, as they call it in Singapore, the A&E, which stands for Accident & Emergency. Upon arrival, patients are immediately triaged into one of four groups. They range from *critically ill* down to *non-emergency*. As you would expect, *critically ill* patients get seen immediately, while *non-emergency* patients may have to wait a while.

But only a *short* while. I can say that because the median wait time between when a patient walks into Singapore General's A&E and when he or she gets seen by a physician is just twenty-one minutes.[2] In those twenty-one minutes, patients get checked in, see a nurse who checks for vitals, and are put into a waiting room to wait for the doctor. And then the doctor walks in. It's quite amazing.

One reason that things move along so quickly is because the Ministry of Health provides real-time feedback about how quickly patients are being processed. In particular, video screens in the A&E waiting room display the wait times for each of the three non-critically ill triage groups. That public display puts salutary pressure on the hospital staff to keep things moving.

I found that pressure to be deeply refreshing. On several occasions, I have had to wait many hours in American emergency rooms. The other patients and I just waited, apparently un-prioritized and seemingly ignored, hour after hour. We would have benefited mightily from first being triaged and then being shown that things were moving along rapidly.

COMMUNITY HOSPITALS AND CHRONIC SICK HOSPITALS

Singapore handles non-acute hospitalization, or "inpatient intermediate-care," with two types of facilities: community hospitals and chronic sick hospitals. *Community hospitals* offer care for patients who are well enough to be discharged from acute-care hospitals but not well enough to go home. They offer twenty-four-hour medical supervision as well as physical and occupational therapy to help get people ready to return home. One example would be a car accident victim who initially needed trauma surgery and intensive care at an acute-care hospital, but now, after being stabilized, needs a few weeks of inpatient convalescent care and physical therapy at a community hospital to be able to function well enough to return home.

By contrast, *chronic sick hospitals* serve mostly elderly patients by providing long-term inpatient nursing care to patients with advanced-stage medical conditions that have left them highly dependent on others. One example would be a patient who has had a tracheostomy on their neck to allow for frequent suctioning of lung secretions.

The most interesting fact about Singapore's chronic sick hospitals, however, is that they are run by non-profit, private-sector philanthropic groups known as Voluntary Welfare Organizations, or VWOs. Some are Catholic, others Muslim or Protestant, still others Buddhist, and others secular. The VWOs manage the facilities, hire and fire staff, and coordinate care with other service providers. For funding, they rely on a mix of private charitable giving and government grants.

It should be noted, however, that the VWOs didn't fall into their role of managing intermediate-care by accident. They were assigned that role by the government, which believes in Aristotle's definition of a nation as a "community of communities." There's more to life than market transactions and government programs. People enjoy helping their fellow citizens and naturally seek to form groups that can make a positive difference in their communities. The government encourages this by giving the VWOs a crucial role to play in the healthcare delivery system and ensuring that they can carry on financially thanks to government grants, which cover about 20 percent of their annual operating budgets.[3]

SINGAPORE'S ELDERLY

The VWOs are also very active in running both home-based hospice services and inpatient nursing homes, which serve elderly people who are too sick for home care but whose illnesses are not severe enough to require hospitalization. The nursing homes offer physical and cognitive therapy and are staffed primarily by gerontologists and other eldercare specialists.

The Ministry of Health has also organized a wide variety of home-based medical and health services to assist elderly persons who may be frail or in need of assistance with everyday tasks. Services include doctors making house calls, home nursing care, meals-on-wheels food delivery, escort and transportation services, and even maid services to help the elderly with their housekeeping.

Neighborhood senior care centers, day care centers for those with dementia, and day rehabilitation centers supplement the home-based services. These facilities allow relatives to drop their elderly parents and grandparents off during working hours. Physical and occupational therapy is provided so that those recovering from strokes and fractures can regain the ability to get around and perform everyday tasks. Those with dementia can get professional supervision and engage in a range of social, recreational, and therapeutic activities. Those in good mental and physical shape can enjoy games, karaoke, handicrafts, and exercise programs. Younger family members can also find support groups and receive training on how to provide quality eldercare at home. The whole point is to allow as many elderly people as possible to continue living at home for as long as possible.

Compared with institutional care, home care is both less expensive and more humane.

SINGAPORE'S CRADLE-TO-GRAVE APPROACH

Now, perhaps you're wondering if Singapore is paying too much attention to the elderly at the expense of the young. Let me share a very telling statistic. Of the 235 public dental clinics run by the government, 221 are located in schools.

This reflects Singapore's cradle-to-grave approach to healthy living. The government's Health Promotion Board organizes and supervises childhood immunizations, hearing and vision tests, and other physical examinations. For adults, the Health Promotion Board has a wide variety of programs, ranging from AIDS education to osteoporosis prevention. The government also makes strong efforts to promote early detection and preventive medicine. Examples include the Community Health Screening program, which encourages people over fifty to get annual screening tests for high blood pressure, diabetes, and high cholesterol levels; the BreastScreen Singapore program, which encourages women over fifty to have a mammogram every two years; and CervicalScreen Singapore, which encourages women ages twenty-five and older to get a Pap smear every three years.

The government supports healthy living in a variety of additional ways. Island-wide greenbelts and park connectors promote walking, running, and relaxation. The Housing Development Board has placed publicly funded gyms in every neighborhood. Community centers disseminate public health and personal wellness information. The Health Promotion Board has made sure that affordable fruits and vegetables are sold in all local markets. And drug abuse is virtually unknown, thanks to the country's draconian anti-drug policies.[4]

WHY WE NEED ACCOUNTABILITY

Crucially, Singapore's public sector has been forced to be competitive—both with itself and with the private sector. The government accomplished this by turning each public hospital into its own nonprofit corporation. While still loosely supervised by the Ministry of Health, each public hospital can organize care as it chooses, hire and fire its own staff, set its own wages and salaries, make its own decisions on how to organize equipment and facilities, and set the prices that it charges for its services.

But, at the same time, pubic hospitals are confronted with a healthcare market in which patients have their choice of many hospitals. So while public hospitals aren't under any pressure to maximize profits, they still have to worry about attracting enough patients to break even. To that end, they must figure out how to be competitive both with each other and with private hospitals.

By contrast, our public hospitals here in the United States lack both competition and financial accountability; if they operate in the red, they simply ask for more taxpayer money. Singapore's public hospitals can't do that. As legally independent nonprofits, they are neither part of the government nor part of its budgeting process. So if they can't break even, they can't ask for government money. What's more, the managers of public hospitals are not government employees. So they know that they have no civil service protections and can get fired if they can't figure out how to break even.

That degree of accountability is exactly the thing we need here in the United States. We need to push back against our third-party payment system's tendency to pass the buck. When individuals know that they themselves must bear the consequences of their decisions, they make better decisions.

Chapter 13

MediSave and the Miraculous 3Ms

Singapore incentivizes both first and second parties to choose prudently, avoid wasteful spending, and innovate. Some of these incentives are market-based, while others are of the central-planning variety. That may seem contradictory, but the government of Singapore is pragmatic. It employs whatever works without wasting time worrying about what people on the left or the right might prefer in their ideal worlds.

I invite you to look at healthcare in the same way. Step back for a moment from whatever presuppositions you may already have about the best way to run a healthcare system *in theory*. Focus instead on the fact that Singapore is running the world's best healthcare system *in practice*.

As you indulge in this exercise, keep in mind that theories usually fail in the real world, so it would be foolish to argue about what works in theory without checking to see what actually works in practice. As Yogi Berra once said, "In theory, there is no difference between theory and practice. In practice, there is." So let us proceed with the wisdom of the Yogi and focus on what works in practice.[1]

What works in practice is a funding system that blends automatic savings, public and private insurance, a fully endowed safety net, and direct government subsidies for the poor. Singapore's healthcare system blends these sources of funding in such a way that individuals have the spending power to engender both competition and efficiency while also enjoying a comprehensive healthcare safety net should they run out of money.

Singapore's Ministry of Health is committed to "ensuring quality and affordable basic medical services for all." In practice, that means delivering high-quality care to everyone, while recognizing that richer people can afford to pay more for their care than poorer people. To that end, public hospitals' wards are divided into different classes that all offer the same level of medical care but differ in terms of amenities, like internet access and cable TV. Everyone receives the same quality of care by the same physicians and nurses, no matter what ward they are staying in, but richer patients are encouraged to pay much more for their accommodations in the fancier wards to help subsidize care for the poorer patients staying in the more spartan wards.[2] In addition, the government grants massive direct subsidies to the poorer patients, so that their bills for any treatment are much lower than those presented to the richer patients staying in the fancier wards.

INTRODUCING THE 3Ms

Once a richer person has received his larger bill and a poorer person has received his smaller bill, the rest of Singapore's unique healthcare financing system comes into play. At the heart of that system lie three integrated programs: MediSave, MediShield, and MediFund—collectively known as the *3Ms*.

- **MediSave** is a mandatory savings program, the proceeds of which are used to pay for future healthcare expenses.
- **MediShield** is a very affordable high-deductible health insurance plan.
- **MediFund** is a social safety net that pays for the healthcare costs of the indigent.

A SYSTEM FOR SAVING

This chapter and the two that follow explain how the 3Ms interact to deliver plenty of money for universal coverage and incentives for first and second parties to keep costs low and improve quality. Let us begin with the 3Ms' financial foundation: MediSave.

MediSave is part of Singapore's automatic savings system, the Central Provident Fund, or CPF. The CPF consists of four mandatory savings accounts into which the average worker is required to save about 35 percent of his or her gross income. The money flows into the four accounts tax-free and remains the personal property of the individual. As personal property, any unspent funds can be willed to heirs. By contrast, the money flowing into the US Social Security and Medicare systems belongs to the government. Any unspent balances are confiscated by Uncle Sam when people die.[3]

The four CPF savings accounts are named the Ordinary Account, the Special Account, the MediSave Account, and the Retirement Account. Up until age fifty-five, a person's entire savings is directed into just the first three accounts (Ordinary, Special, and MediSave). Once a person reaches fifty-five, the Ordinary and Special Accounts are combined to form the person's Retirement Account. From that age onward, each person only has only two accounts: the MediSave Account and the Retirement Account.

People can invest their CPF savings balances in a wide variety of
private-sector investments, including stocks, bonds, real estate, gold,
mutual funds, and insurance savings vehicles like whole life insurance.
Each of those private investments is exposed to some degree of market
risk, so the government also offers CPF savers the chance to invest in
special Singapore government bonds that offer a guaranteed minimum
return.

The minimum return depends on the type of account. Ordinary
Account balances that are invested into these special bonds are guaranteed a minimum return of 2.5 percent per year. The return is even
better for any Special Account, MediSave Account, or Retirement
Account balances that are invested into these bonds. They are guaranteed a minimum return of 4 percent per year. But that's not all. If
the short-term interest rate paid by local banks is higher than the
minimum rate, investors earn that higher short-term rate. In this way,
the special bonds give savers a chance for upside without any worry
about downside.

If that wasn't impressive enough, perhaps this will excite you:
when Singapore runs a budget surplus, the government distributes a
large chunk of the excess into people's CPF accounts. And surplus or
no surplus, the government creates a MediSave Account for each
newborn and deposits S$3,000 into the account to provide some
health-financing security for each child right from the get-go.[4]

Up until age fifty-five, the majority of each person's mandatory
savings flows into his or her Ordinary Account. That makes sense,
because Ordinary Account balances can only be spent on things that
are priorities for adults in their prime earning years: housing purchases, educational expenses, and insurance premiums. Thanks to
those Ordinary Accounts, young and middle-aged Singaporeans have
plenty of dough to pay for down payments on homes, college tuition,
vocational instruction, and insurance. The transformative nature of

giving people that sort of accumulated purchasing power at a young age can be understood by noting that nearly everyone in Singapore saves enough money for a down payment on a mortgage. As a result, Singapore's home ownership rate is the world's highest, 91 percent.[5] By contrast, the US home ownership rate hovers around 65 percent—in large part because many Americans never save enough money for a down payment.[6]

The ability to spend Ordinary Account balances on education also means that Singapore's workers nearly always have the money necessary to go back to school and retrain for another career when industries die or companies shut down. By contrast, the average American caught up in that sort of situation has no ready savings at hand. Forty percent of Americans cannot even cover an unexpected expense of $400.[7] They are forced to either forgo the retraining they need or take out student loans to pay for it.

As mentioned above, the portion of an individual's savings that does not flow into his Ordinary Account flows instead into his Special and MediSave Accounts. The money in the Special Account is earmarked for retirement and can't be touched until the individual turns fifty-five and his Special and Ordinary Accounts are combined to form his Retirement Account (from which he can start drawing at age fifty-five).

THE SECURITY OF SAVINGS

Regardless of a person's age, money directed into a MediSave Account can only be spent on healthcare, either for the individual himself or for the individual's family. Allowable expenditures include MediShield insurance premiums, inpatient hospital treatments, and selected outpatient treatments like chemotherapy and radiation. MediSave balances can also be used to pay the premiums for

ElderCare, Singapore's insurance plan for long-term care and assisted living.

Because most people are quite healthy into their fifties, money rapidly accumulates in most people's MediSave Accounts. And because the amount of mandatory savings that flows into MediSave Accounts runs between 6 and 9 percent of annual income (depending on age), Singaporeans usually enjoy three or so decades of accumulated healthcare savings before old age begins to take its toll and healthcare spending ramps up. As of 2014, there were 3.2 million MediSave Accounts with an average balance of S$21,800—enough for ten acute hospital admissions for indigent patients receiving government subsidies.[8]

The combined size of the 3.2 million accounts is staggering. In 2014, they totaled S$70.5 billion, or about 18.1 percent of Singapore's 2014 GDP of S$390.1 billion. To put that in perspective, recall that Singapore's annual healthcare bill comes to 4.2 percent of GDP. So the total amount of money in Singapore's MediSave Accounts would be enough to fund Singapore's entire healthcare system for nearly four and a half years without having to obtain even a single penny of funding from any other source. That is real security—the kind that is hard to imagine in America, where the Medicare and Medicaid trust funds are massively underfunded (along with Social Security and most private and public pension plans).

But, believe it or not, there can be such a thing as too much security. Because Singapore's collective pile of health savings was becoming excessive relative to the country's likely future medical expenses, Singapore's government imposed a ceiling on MediSave Account balances. That ceiling currently stands at S$49,800 per person. Any additional saving that would have normally flowed into a person's MediSave Account is instead directed towards their retirement, either through the Special Account if the person is under fifty-five or the Retirement Account if the person is fifty-five or older.

But let's stop for a few seconds to reflect on something magical.

Take a deep breath or two, then sit in a state of bewildered awe as you contemplate the fact that Singapore needed to impose a cap on MediSave balances. Has any other country ever designed a health-care financing system that had a tendency toward accumulating *too much money* for future health expenses? Has any other country ever had to worry that it was *over-saving* for healthcare?

The answer, of course, is no. But as one of my friends commented: *Over-savings? That's a good problem to have!*

Just how good only becomes apparent when you realize that Singapore's high quality and low costs are the result of all that sav-ings. Indeed, it is only because of the money in their MediSave Accounts that Singapore's citizens have so much control over both their own individual healthcare and over the overall healthcare sys-tem as a whole. Their accumulated purchasing power allows them to shop around for the best deal. The fact that citizens can take their MediSave money elsewhere forces second parties to relentlessly inno-vate to improve quality and reduce costs. And, as I will show you in the next chapter, MediSave balances directly fund the premiums and copays of the high-deductible MediShield insurance system that frees Singapore's citizens from having to worry about being bankrupted by catastrophically expensive medical conditions.

Chapter 14

MediShield and the Right Incentives

MediShield is a low-cost catastrophic health insurance plan which can be used at any public hospital or clinic in Singapore. Run by the CPF, it covers hospitalization expenses and a variety of expensive outpatient treatments, including kidney dialysis, chemotherapy, and radiation treatments.

Participation in MediShield was voluntary from the program's inception in the early 1990s through 2015, when MediShield expanded into MediShield Life, which required cradle-to-grave participation. I will discuss the innovations made by MediShield Life in detail in Chapter 20, but here is a key point that must be made regarding the original, pre-2015 MediShield program that I discuss in this chapter: the vast majority of Singaporeans were enrolled, even though the program was purely voluntary. In 2013, for instance, 3.6 million people, or 94 percent of Singapore's residents, were enrolled in MediShield either as policyholders or as dependents of policyholders.[1]

Of those 3.6 million people, 2.4 million opted to pay extra for supplementary Integrated Shield plans that offered additional benefits and coverage, while one million people opted to pay extra for an ElderShield plan that covered long-term eldercare.

COVERAGE THAT FACILITATES COMPETITION

Both MediShield and MediShield life work in conjunction with the money people have saved in their MediSave Accounts, since MediSave balances can be used to pay for MediShield's premiums, deductibles, and copays.

MediShield has a S$2,000 annual deductible. Until policyholders reach that limit, their healthcare spending comes entirely out of pocket, either from their MediSave Accounts or any other source of money that they might want to use instead. The S$2,000 annual deductible is critically important, because it incentivizes first parties to weigh costs against benefits and thereby avoid wasteful spending. Out-of-pocket spending below the annual deductible also creates a booming, competitive market for healthcare services. Because each doctor and each hospital knows that patients are free to take their money elsewhere, they must compete to deliver both high quality and low prices.

The benefits of free markets and competition are maximized, however, only when consumers have good information on which to base their decisions. To that end, the Ministry of Health posts cost-comparison data on the internet so consumers can make informed choices. For the most common hospital procedures, people can look up both the 50th percentile and 90th percentile total bill sizes (which include even extraneous costs like room and board). For surgical procedures, people can drill down even more and get percentile cost data that excludes those extraneous costs.

To see how that information facilitates informed comparison shopping, suppose that I live in Singapore and am in need of a knee replacement. I would begin my shopping expedition by calling up several orthopedic surgeons to get quotes. Then, using the cost data posted to the internet, I could compare those quoted prices with the 50th percentile and 90th percentile prices from across the entire country to see if the quotes I collected were competitively priced. I would then ask around to see which surgeons are well respected by their peers and highly recommended by their patients. By doing so, I can identify the provider who offers me the most attractive combination of price and quality.

I might first see that Surgeon A is quoting a lower price than Surgeon B. But then I might also find that Surgeon A is not as highly recommended by former patients as Surgeon B. With those facts in mind, I might select Surgeon B, despite the higher price. Other consumers would of course be free to select Surgeon A and his lower price. That might strike you as dangerous, but it allows each consumer to act as his or her own judge in what we might refer to, legalistically, as the case of *"Quality v. Price."* It also forces providers to care about both of those factors simultaneously. If providers get lazy on either one, consumers will condemn them, withdraw their business, and consign them to bankruptcy.

By contrast, that feedback mechanism is mostly absent in America, because our system of third-party payments tends to obscure information about both price and quality. The result is a system deprived of competition. Our second-party providers are *not* under constant pressure to provide lower prices and higher quality. Because they are paid by third parties, our second parties don't have to worry about whether first parties feel they are getting a good deal on either price or quality. When Americans deal with the case of *Quality v.*

Price, court is never convened, decisions are never rendered, and the guilty are never condemned to bankruptcy.

KEEPING SOME SKIN IN THE GAME

Singapore designed MediShield so that the judgment of consumers applies not only to the S$2,000 worth of spending that occurs before people hit the annual deductible, but also to any spending above the S$2,000 annual deductible. That's because there are 10 to 20 percent copays on all medical spending above S$2,000.

For medical spending between S$2,000 per year and S$3,000 per year (that is, on any spending from the S$2,000 annual deductible up to S$3,000 per year), there is a 20 percent copay. For any spending from S$3,000 per year up to S$5,000 per year, there is a 15 percent copay. And for any spending above S$5,000 per year, there is a 10 percent copay.

To see how that tiered copay system works in practice, suppose it's June 3 and you haven't spent any money yet on healthcare this year. But on June 3, you get hit by a car while walking across the street.[2] The car hits you just above your left knee and your doctor explains that you will need some arthroscopic knee surgery to repair a torn meniscus. After shopping around, you decide to go with a surgeon who will charge S$4,500. Under MediShield, the first S$2,000 would come out of your own pocket, since you have a S$2,000 annual deductible. You can pay that S$2,000 out of your MediSave money. Then, for the remaining S$2,500, you would be required to pay 20 percent of the amount between S$2,000 and S$3,000 and 15 percent of the amount from S$3,000 to S$4,500. That comes to a total of S$425 (= S$200 for the 20 percent copay on the thousand dollars between S$2,000 and S$3,000 + S$225 for the 15 percent copay on the fifteen hundred dollars between S$3,000 and S$4,500). The remaining S$2,075 of the amount from S$2,000 to S$4,500 would be paid by MediShield. Thus, even after people have hit their annual deductible, they are always faced with a share of the total cost. This incentivizes them to weigh costs and benefits in all situations.

By contrast, many Americans have low deductibles coupled with modest copays that extend only up to a few thousand dollars in annual spending. After that, any additional spending falls entirely on the third-party insurance company—at which point insured individuals lose any financial incentive to eliminate wasteful spending or to care about finding a low cost, high-quality provider.

Incentives are even worse for people with Medicare, Medicaid, or Veteran's Administration health benefits because these programs have little-to-no cost sharing with patients. All or most of the bill falls on the government; from the very first dollar of spending, individuals have little-to-no financial incentive to spend prudently or shop around for the best deal.

Singapore avoids that moral hazard problem by making sure that people have money to spend on healthcare *and* the financial incentives to spend that money prudently. MediSave ensures that they have money to spend, while MediShield's deductible and copay structure ensures that first parties always have some "skin in the game." Faced with these incentives, first parties shop around and, by doing so, force second parties to figure out ways to deliver high quality at low prices.

First parties are also confronted by the real cost of healthcare in another way. They have to pay their own MediShield premiums. They can do that with money from their MediSave Accounts, but at no time are they under the illusion that health insurance is free. The premium costs them. The deductible costs them. The copay costs them. And, if they use MediSave to pay for those expenses, they see every dollar required for those three payments being removed—permanently—from their MediSave Accounts.

POLITICALLY INDEPENDENT ADMINISTRATION

For those of you who have a keen dislike for private health insurance companies, I should emphasize that MediShield is run entirely by the CPF, which takes all the associated actuarial risks onto its own balance sheet. In running MediShield, the CPF decides the size of the annual deductible as well as the percentages and thresholds for the copays. As a non-elected body, the CPF can decide what is and is not covered by MediShield without having to worry about the special-interest lobbying that plagues state insurance regulators here in the United States. Coverage is limited to hospitalization for medically necessary treatments as well as expensive outpatient procedures. Viagra is not included—and neither are the Hoveround personal mobility scooters discussed in an earlier chapter.

The government has also set daily, annual, and lifetime limits on MediShield claims so as to keep a lid on prices by discouraging wasteful spending. Consider MediShield's daily limit on ward charges (the room and board part of a hospital stay). They are capped at S$900 per day, so providers have an incentive to provide ward services at that price or less. The cap also gives patients a personal financial disincentive against lavish spending, because any ward charges above the daily limit come out of the patient's MediSave Account or other personal sources of cash. The annual and lifetime claims limits—of S$70,000 and S$300,000, respectively—serve a similar purpose. They remind people that MediShield is not a bottomless common pool from which they can withdraw other people's money to pay for their own healthcare. Any spending beyond the claims limits must be paid entirely out of their own savings.

The CPF also highly regulates the Integrated Shield health insurance policies offered by private insurance companies. These policies augment a policyholder's coverage relative to what he could file claims for under MediShield. A few examples include Integrated Shield policies that pay for nicer wards in public hospitals, cover the costs of a wider variety of medical procedures, and reimburse for medical treatments performed in private hospitals and clinics (whereas MediShield only covers treatments in public facilities). Integrated Shield plans also allow for unlimited lifetime claims.

Two points need to be made about these supplemental health insurance plans. First, the only way that anybody can get into an Integrated Shield plan is if they first pay for MediShield coverage. That is very important, because it prevents private insurance companies from cherry picking the healthier people and leaving only the sickly in the MediShield insurance pool.

Second, the private insurance companies that offer Integrated Shield plans have to aggressively compete on premiums (rather than coverage options), because the government only allows minor differences in what each policy covers and in how each of them structures deductibles and copays. The government also limits the number of Integrated Shield plans to a half dozen or so in order to avoid information overload on the part of consumers.

SHOCKINGLY LOW PREMIUMS

But enough with the details behind MediShield.

It's time for the big reveal. It's time to show you just how little MediShield costs.

Keep in mind that MediShield wouldn't be very attractive if it was hideously expensive. What would be the point if it cost so much that people would rather do without it? And what would be the point if it was bankrupting the nation, as is the case with US health insurance?

To put things in stark perspective, note that the average annual premium for an individual health insurance plan in the United States was $6,025 in 2014 (the final year that traditional MediShield was in effect before Singapore transitioned to MediShield Life). Well, back in 2014 you could go online to the Singapore Ministry of Health's website and compare that number with annual individual MediShield premiums.

The MediShield premiums did vary by age, but they were shockingly low for all age groups. As you look at the following numbers, note that I am giving them to you in Singapore dollars (S$) and that, at 2014 exchange rates, one Singapore dollar equaled 80 cents worth of US money (i.e., S$1.00 = $0.80).

For those twenty and under, the annual premium for MediShield insurance coverage was all of S$50 per year. Once you convert that into US dollars, it's even less expensive; it equals just $40 per year in US currency.

Premiums *do* increase for older individuals, but, even for the elderly, they are still shockingly affordable. The premium is S$66 per year for twenty-one- to thirty-year-olds; S$105 per year for thirty-one- to forty-year-olds; S$220 per year for forty-one- to fifty-year-olds; S$345 per year for fifty-one- to sixty-year-olds; S$455 for sixty-one- to sixty-five-year-olds; S$540 per year for sixty-six- to seventy-year-olds; and so on up to S$1,190 for eighty-six- to ninety-year-olds.

So even for the very elderly, who are prone to running up lots of medical costs, annual premiums are still wondrously low compared with US health insurance premiums. The S$1,190 premium for eighty-six- to ninety-year-olds translates into just $952 in US dollars. That's 85 percent less than the average US individual health insurance premium of $6,025.

The percentage discounts are, of course, even larger for younger people. As an example, I turned forty-one in 2014. My S$220 MediShield premium would have equaled $176 of US currency—or

97 percent less than the average cost of an individual health insurance policy in the United States that year.

That would have made a very nice birthday present. Too bad I live in America.

If you are wondering how MediShield premiums can be so low, remember that the 3M system demands high deductibles and meaningful copays. That creates competition, which in turn leads to low prices. So when MediShield has to pay its portion of any spending above the annual deductible, it can do so at extremely low prices. Whereas insurance companies have to pay nosebleed prices for healthcare services in the United States, MediShield is making its claims reimbursements in the lowest-cost healthcare system in the developed world.

As one example of just how low-cost that system is, a heart bypass surgery that will run you about $130,000 in the United States can be had in Singapore for just $18,000, or about 76 percent less. A hip replacement costs 62 percent less. A heart valve is 92 percent less. And, by the way, these are the unsubsidized, full-freight prices charged to foreigners by private Singapore hospitals. Indigent locals can get them for far less at public hospitals, thanks to the direct subsidy program that I will discuss in a couple of chapters.[3]

One final point should be made about MediShield: it is self-reinforcing and self-perpetuating. By demanding high deductibles and meaningful copays, MediShield creates the competition necessary to reduce prices. Those lower prices lead to the low premiums that induce mass participation. And with so many participating, you get the strong competition and low prices that allow for low premiums.

Heck, the prices are so cheap that even Integrated Shield plans are comically inexpensive. Believe it or not, the most expensive Integrated Shield plan, the Aviva MyShield Plan 1, only charges a premium of S$687 *per year* for a middle-aged guy like me. In return, I get coverage that includes private as well as public hospital stays; a S$650,000 annual claims limit; an unlimited lifetime claims limit; an additional S$150,000 per year claims allowance for critical illnesses; unlimited "as charged" compensation for everything from daily ward and treatment charges to surgery, kidney dialysis, cancer treatments, and major organ transplants; as well as ninety days each of both pre- and post-hospitalization coverage and a lifetime waiver from paying premiums if I become permanently disabled.

That plan—the most expensive one in Singapore!—is, in fact, so *in*expensive by American standards that the only way to make it look pricey is to point out how much it charges the *extremely* elderly. Its annual premium is S$8,483 per year...for anybody one hundred years old or older. For *anybody* younger, the premium for Singapore's most expensive individual health insurance plan is massively less than the $6,025 that Americans on average get charged for middling coverage by a middling plan.

As with much else about our healthcare system, that's *very* embarrassing.

Chapter 15

MediShield Encourages Participation and Fairness with Age-Rated Insurance

MediShield's premiums are age-rated rather than community-rated, which means MediShield charges different premiums to different age groups, rather than lumping the entire population together and charging everybody the same premium. Singapore's use of age rating has achieved high voluntary participation rates and protection for the poor while avoiding the adverse-selection problem (which is the tendency for only the sickest people to opt into an insurance system while healthier people opt out). Age rating also prevents politicians from using a nation's health insurance system as a way of facilitating massive intergenerational wealth transfers from young to old.

Because MediShield was voluntary before it morphed into MediShield Life in 2015, it had to ensure not only that its premiums attracted a large number of voluntary participants, but also that those participants collectively paid enough in premiums to cover their future collective health insurance claims.

To see how this could go wrong, consider a voluntary system that charges two prices: a high premium for the young and a low premium for the elderly. In setting up the system, the actuaries who crunch the numbers set the premiums for the two groups on the assumption that everybody in the country will volunteer to sign up. If that were to happen, enough money would be collected in premiums to pay out on all future healthcare claims.

But, given that the system is voluntary, will everyone actually sign up? The answer is no. The young understand that they are much healthier than the old, so they will balk at having to pay high rates; they thereby won't subsidize the much higher healthcare spending of the elderly. On the other hand, the old will love the low rates that they are offered. They will sign up in droves.

The result will be adverse selection, with only the old (and costly) signing up. The insurance system will be insolvent, not collecting nearly enough in premiums from its elderly enrollees to cover their healthcare costs. At the same time, you will also have millions of young people uninsured and susceptible to bankruptcy if stricken with a serious illness that generates high medical expenses.

A voluntary system is also likely to collapse under the weight of adverse selection if it uses a community rating and charges everyone exactly the same premium. Why? Because in that case, the young and healthy will again flee as they figure out that, while the premium is the same for everyone on the front end, the claims flow on the back end is heavily biased toward the elderly. Community rating will tend to fail in any voluntary system that enrolls participants with different cost profiles.

If you are, however, politically or ideologically committed to charging everyone the same premium, there is a simple solution to the adverse selection issues that result from community rating: you can make participation mandatory. If everyone is compelled into signing up and paying in (as was attempted by the Affordable Care Act with its fines on individuals who did not purchase health insurance), then you do not need to worry about any individual or group deciding not to participate. With everyone forced to pay whatever you decide to charge, your only constraint as a policy-maker is to make sure that the total inflow of premiums is sufficient to pay out on all future claims (and even that constraint won't matter if you are willing to subsidize the whole system with tax revenues obtained from other sources).

Because MediShield was established as a voluntary system, its designers couldn't get around the adverse-selection problem by forcing everyone to participate. They had to design a premium structure that would be attractive to both young and old, sick and healthy. The method they chose was age rating, under which the premium of each age cohort (for example, twenty- to thirty-year-olds) is set to reflect its own costs and risks. That staggered premium structure avoids the adverse-selection problem because each cohort will collectively get back what its members have collectively paid in. Nobody will be overcharged to subsidize the members of another cohort.

Because younger people are typically so much healthier than older people, MediShield's age-rated premiums are much lower for younger cohorts. As noted earlier, those under twenty years of age pay only S$50 per year, while premiums are S$345 per year for fifty-one- to sixty-year-olds and S$1,190 for those in their late eighties. This premium structure encourages voluntary participation across all age groups, because the members of each cohort are presented with premiums that reflect the actual healthcare costs and risks of people like themselves.

Please note that MediShield achieved a 94 percent voluntary participation rate with this age-rated premium structure. This extremely high rate of voluntary participation should give pause to those who insist that every country must make insurance participation mandatory. In 2009, when the healthcare debates leading up to the passage of the Affordable Care Act were taking place, only 84 percent of Americans had health insurance.[1] So Singapore's use of age rating proves that you can achieve a much higher rate of health insurance enrollment in a properly designed voluntary system than what the United States managed to achieve in its poorly structured, employment-based system before the ACA started using fines in its attempt to enforce 100 percent participation. It is also important to point out that even after the Affordable Care Act was fully implemented, its fines were insufficient in achieving the ACA's goal of universal health insurance coverage. In 2017, fully three years after the ACA was fully implemented, only 91.2 percent of Americans had health insurance. Thus, MediShield's 94 percent voluntary participation rate stands well ahead of what the ACA was able to achieve, even after several years of fining those who did not want to participate.

It is also extremely important to note that the six percent of Singaporeans who did not have MediShield coverage are believed to have been well-off people who opted to rely exclusively on employer-provided health insurance or who were wealthy enough to self-insure. So while Singapore may have had a 6 percent non-participation rate for MediShield, those who voluntarily opted out were in quite different circumstances than the 16 percent of Americans who did not have health insurance in 2009 when the Affordable Care Act was being debated, or the 8.8 percent who did not have health insurance in 2017, three years after the ACA had been fully implemented.

Those Americans were, for the most part, poor, unemployed, or underemployed. They did not have access to health insurance because they had lost their employer-sponsored health insurance or they were poor—but not poor enough to qualify for Medicaid or other types of government-sponsored health insurance. So when you look at the 6 percent non-participation rate of the original version of MediShield, you should think of it as reflecting success rather than failure. Singapore's voluntary health insurance system managed to achieve mass participation and include the vulnerable while also collecting enough in premiums to guarantee its payouts. It's hardly a problem that a well-off 6 percent decided to get their healthcare elsewhere.

MediShield's use of age-rated premiums also prevents Singapore's politicians from using the nation's health insurance system as a vehicle for intergenerational wealth-transfers. With MediShield, annual premiums for each cohort are based on taking in enough money to cover exactly one year's healthcare spending for the members of that cohort. Each cohort therefore pays in only enough to take care of the other members of its cohort. There is no transfer of wealth from one group to another by making one group's premiums artificially high in order to make another group's premiums artificially low.

By contrast, the Affordable Care Act utilizes community-rated premiums, with younger cohorts forced to pay vastly more in insurance premiums than they will file in insurance claims. Their overpayments subsidize the members of older cohorts, who pay massively less each year than the cost of their care. Now, you may think that such a system is fair, as the young people who are overpaying today will eventually become elderly people who get to underpay several decades from now. But if you assume that, you are also assuming that politicians will be able to ensure the future solvency of the system.

I am dubious about that assumption. Politicians throughout the world have overpromised and under-delivered with both old-age pension plans and national healthcare systems. The pressure to win the next election makes politicians heavily biased towards overpromising today and underfunding tomorrow. I see no reason to believe that the young, who today are being forced to overpay under the

Affordable Care Act, will actually get it all back when they are older. It's much more likely that they will get only a small fraction of what they've been promised. If you share that opinion, you will see yet another reason to emulate Singapore's use of age rating for determining health insurance premiums: age rating prevents mendacious politicians from using a nation's health insurance system to facilitate intergenerational wealth transfers that won't end up being repaid.

Let me close this short chapter by pointing out that MediShield's use of age rating also prevents politicians from running a nation's health insurance system like a Ponzi scheme. To see the problem, consider the strange case of Ida May Fuller, the first person to ever receive a Social Security check. As with other early recipients of Social Security, she had only paid in three years' worth of payroll taxes, amounting to a combined total of $22.75, before she began to receive Social Security benefits at age sixty-five. She then lived to age one hundred, collecting a total of $22,888.92 in Social Security benefits.[2]

As with the other early recipients of Social Security, she didn't pay in nearly as much as she took out. How was that possible? Because Social Security isn't really a savings system. It's a wealth-transfer system from the young to the old that uses payroll taxes obtained from the current crop of workers to fund benefits for the current crop of retirees. Ida May Fuller got $22,888.92 after paying in just $22.75, because younger workers were picking up the tab.

Unfortunately, with falling birth rates, there won't be enough younger workers paying in to Social Security in coming decades to keep all the promises that have been made to older workers and retirees. When that happens, Social Security will teeter on the brink of collapse, just like a Ponzi scheme does when withdrawals begin to exceed deposits.

Ida May Fuller's ability to pull out more than she put in was equivalent to being one of the early investors in a Ponzi scheme. Future generations won't be so lucky. They will pay in when they are young, but then find the Ponzi scheme in default when they are older and their benefits come due.

Fortunately for Singapore, that fraudulent Ponzi design is not possible with MediShield. MediShield does not make long-term promises based on short-run funding. Its age-rated premiums restrict it to operating one year at a time, with the premiums paid in by each cohort each year fully funding that year's payouts.

Because MediShield fully funds all its promises, nobody has to fear being the last guy paying in to a Ponzi scheme before it collapses.

Chapter 16

MediFund and Direct Subsidies: Singapore's Amazing Healthcare Safety Net

MediFund is the final component of Singapore's healthcare safety net—or, more precisely, the final component of Singapore's safety net for *financing* healthcare. If an indigent person finds himself unable to afford his medical bills despite MediSave and MediShield, he can apply to MediFund to pay for his healthcare costs.

But before explaining how MediFund is organized and how it distributes funds to those who have run out of money, it is important that I first describe the direct subsidy program which subsidizes the healthcare bills of the needy so that they are very unlikely to ever run out of money to begin with. Thanks to that direct subsidy program, MediFund is only rarely needed.

The direct subsidy program uses general tax revenues to provide grants to Singapore's public hospitals and clinics. Those direct subsidies allow them to offer subsidized prices to their poorer patients. The subsidies reach as much as 80 percent of total bill size for those with the greatest need.

The total volume of direct subsidy funding is significant, amounting to 12 percent of all healthcare spending in Singapore in 2012. In terms of Singapore's healthcare safety net, the direct subsidy program is important because it preemptively removes some of the funding pressure from the 3Ms, since the subsidized prices make it much less likely that a poorer person will run out of MediSave money. By subsidizing prices in advance, direct subsidies establish a pay-it-forward safety net that is in place even before patients have health issues and need to make payments.

Even better, the government has come up with a clever way to ensure that subsidized prices are utilized by only the neediest. As will be explained in more detail in the next chapter, Singapore's public hospitals have a variety of types of wards available, some with more creature comforts and some with less. The doctors, nurses, and quality of care are identical in all wards, but prices are substantially higher for patients staying in the comfy wards. Those higher prices cause a natural self-selection to take place, with richer patients typically opting for the comfier wards while poorer patients elect to stay in the more spartan (but far less expensive) wards.

That self-sorting is extremely useful for two reasons. First, the richer patients end up voluntarily opting to pay higher prices, and the hospital can then recycle those higher payments into subsidizing prices for poorer patients. Second, the self-sorting of the poor into the less luxurious wards means that hospitals can target direct subsidy funds at those less luxurious wards, further reducing bill sizes for the poorer patients staying there.

I must reiterate that *all patients get the same level of medical care* no matter what class of ward they are staying in. A rich surgery inpatient who opts to pay a lot to stay in his own room will get the *same* surgery by the *same* surgeon as a low-income inpatient who opts to pay very little to share a subsidized ward with eight other patients. Thus, Singapore has found a very clever way to subsidize public hospitals, such that the well-off are unlikely to receive any benefit from the direct subsidy program. With rich and poor self-selecting into different wards, public hospitals can focus their direct subsidies at the people who really need the help: the poor.

I should also re-emphasize that public hospital physicians are paid fixed annual salaries. As a result, they have no financial incentive to cater to the rich in any way. Thus, the quality of treatment ends up being the same, despite rich patients being charged more than poor patients.

MEDIFUND

Let's now return to our discussion of MediFund. MediFund is the nickname for the Medical Endowment Fund established by the government of Singapore in 1993. The endowment currently contains over S$4.5 billion that is invested in a wide variety of assets. The returns generated by those investments are directed toward covering the healthcare costs of the indigent.[1] An additional endowment fund, known as MediFund Silver, was created in 2007 to provide additional funding for the indigent elderly.

The interest generated by the MediFund endowment flows as grants to approved public healthcare facilities including hospitals, polyclinics, and nursing homes. Those who apply have to be subsidized patients (i.e., patients who are already receiving direct subsidies due to financial need). Then, they must additionally demonstrate that they would have difficulty affording their subsidized bills despite MediSave and MediShield.

Medical social workers (MSWs) are available at each MediFund-approved facility to help the indigent navigate the system, fill out paperwork, and demonstrate that they would suffer financial hardship if they were made to pay on their own. The medical social workers ensure that somebody inside the system is there to advocate for the indigent.

To ensure local control and community mindfulness, the ultimate authority to approve applications at each facility lies with a MediFund Committee that consists of independent volunteers who are actively involved in social work in the local community. However, applications can be approved at a variety of different levels, depending on how straightforward they are in terms of meeting the Ministry of Health's general approval criteria.[2] As related by Singapore healthcare expert Jeremy Lim:

> Upon social worker assessment of patient's eligibility, the application will escalate to the approving level, which could be head of the Medical Social Worker Department, the CFO (Chief Financial Officer) or the Medifund Committee. Eligibility could be either straightforward or non-straightforward. Straightforward cases can be approved on the very day and will normally take about 30 minutes tops of the MSW's time. Non-straightforward cases could take about 45-60 minutes, not including a report that is needed to justify the quantum of assistance. Those [highly unusual] cases that need Medifund Committee approval normally tend to wait for about three weeks or more, depending on when the next [Medifund Committee] meeting is convened. Repeat applications, also known as review cases, will normally take about 15 minutes, provided circumstantial changes are minimal or none. Normal procedure is to furnish the Medifund form again, with recent documents for support.[3]

Please note just how quick and efficient the MediFund system is. The vast majority of cases get approved in under an hour; the rest have to wait, in most cases, no longer than about a month until the next meeting of the local MediFund Committee.

Even better, over 99 percent of applications are approved and, of those approved, 93 percent receive full assistance, meaning that MediFund pays for 100 percent of the patient's outstanding subsidized bill.[4] As a result, poorer Singaporeans can have confidence that MediFund isn't just an empty promise. If they run out of money to pay for healthcare, MediFund will almost certainly approve their applications for financial assistance.

Singapore's overall healthcare safety net is amazing because of how little the final MediFund component gets used. Now, it's true that 1,006,000 MediFund applications (including MediFund Silver) were approved in 2014 for both inpatient and outpatient care. That may seem like a lot, but they totaled just S$157.5 million. As a result, MediFund accounted for only about 0.8 percent of Singapore's total healthcare spending in 2014.[5] That implies that the rest of the country's healthcare financing system works so well that the final stage of its healthcare safety net accounts for under 1 percent of national healthcare spending.

Viewed from the hospital and clinic level, the low rate at which MediFund must be tapped for funds is equally remarkable. The director of one of Singapore's major public hospitals told me that only 1.4 percent of all revenue received by his hospital came from MediFund.

An even deeper appreciation of how little MediFund is actually utilized can be gained when you remember that Singapore's current cohort of elderly citizens didn't get a chance to save very much under MediSave because they were already middle-aged or elderly when Singapore created MediSave. Consider a person who is now eighty-five. They were already in their fifties when MediSave started in 1985.

As a result, they only had a few years of employment during which they could accumulate MediSave money for future healthcare expenses. Thus, there is a much higher likelihood that they will eventually run out of MediSave money as compared to people who were, say, twenty-five years old in 1985, and who as a result spent most of their working years putting money into their MediSave Accounts.

The fact that MediFund spending represents just 0.8 percent of all medical spending in Singapore is consequently even more extraordinary, because it means that MediSave and MediFund are holding up despite all the elderly residents who had only a few years to accumulate money in their Medisave Accounts before retiring. Looking to the future, that pressure will decrease as the population ages and the current cohort of elderly are replaced by later cohorts who were able to save into MediSave for most or all of their working years.

By contrast, the US institution that funds healthcare for the elderly—Medicare—is heading for both near-term as well as long-term fiscal catastrophe. The Medicare trust fund is set to run dry in 2026.[6] And looking out over a seventy-five-year timeframe, Medicare's expected outlays exceed its expected income by $37 trillion, or about $112,000 per person currently living in the United States.[7] So our system for providing the elderly with healthcare isn't just inefficient and expensive; it's unsustainable.

That's yet another reason to look very closely at Singapore and its savings-driven healthcare funding system. Individuals save for future expenses with MediSave while the government saves for future expenses with MediFund. Together, the programs provide ample funding not only for Singapore's current healthcare needs, but for its future needs as well.

Chapter 17

Singapore's Multiple Ward Classes: Healthcare, Not Hotels

Many would feel comforted to hear that rich and poor Singaporeans receive exactly the same medical care by exactly the same doctors and nurses when staying in Singapore's public hospitals. But Americans tend to be startled by how significantly the various classes of hospital wards accessed by the rich and poor differ in terms of creature comforts.

The nicest wards in each public hospital are named Class A1+ and Class A1. Next down the line come B1 wards, then B2+ and B2 wards, and then, finally, Class C wards. At the largest public hospital, Singapore General, 2018 ward prices ranged from S$466.52 per day for an A1+ ward all the way down to just S$35 per day for a bed in a Class C ward.

Richer Singaporeans tend to shun the S$35 per day Class C wards because they are big open rooms shared by nine patients at a time. The Class C wards are also naturally ventilated—meaning no air conditioning. Singapore lies just eighty-five miles north of the equator and hence has the same balmy climate year-round. So

Class C wards simply keep the windows open all year long. Figure 17.1 is a picture of one side of a Class C ward at National University Hospital.

Figure 17.1: A Class C Ward at National University Hospital

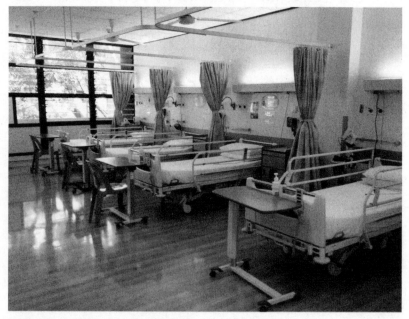

Source: National University Hospital website, http://www.nuh.com.sg.

Naturally, people who can easily afford more will usually be eager to avoid sharing a room with eight other people and having to go without air conditioning in the year-round tropical heat. The average high temperature in Singapore is 89 degrees every day of the year and it's humid, too. So, if you have a little extra money, you will likely opt for a B2 ward, which has only six beds in a big room, plus ceiling fans, and semi-automated electronic beds. That will run you S$79 per day.

For S$140 per day, you can get yourself into a B2+ ward, which has only five beds, air conditioning, and an attached bathroom and toilet so you don't have to walk down the hallway to shower or use the facilities.

If that still isn't luxurious enough for you, you can opt to spend $251.45 per night for a B1 ward, which has only 4 beds, air conditioning, an attached bathroom and toilet, semi-automatic beds, plus individual televisions, telephones, and your choice of meals. Figure 17.2 is picture of a B1 ward at Changi General Hospital.

Figure 17.2: A Class B1 Ward at Changi General Hospital

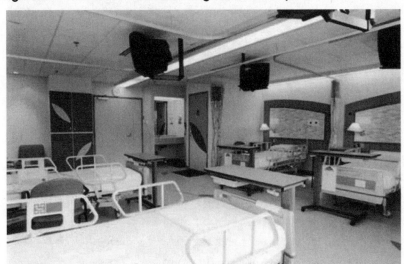

Source: Changi General Hospital website, http://www.cgh.com.sg.

The A1+ and A1 wards can charge S$466.52 and S$422.65, respectively, because they offer air-conditioned single rooms with private bathrooms and toilets, hotel-style toiletries, your own TV and telephone, a fully automatic bed, and your choice of meals. They also have mini-fridges, sofa beds, and complimentary Wi-Fi. Figure 17.3 is a picture of an A1 Ward at KK Women's and Children's Hospital.

Figure 17.3: A Class A1 Ward (Single Room) at KK Women's and Children's Hospital

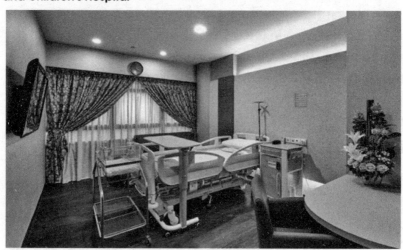

Source: KK Women's and Children's Hospital website, http://www.kkh.com.sg.

The difference between the A1 and A1+ wards is that the A1+ wards are two-room suites that are, additionally, designed to look like apartments rather than hospital rooms. There's full carpeting, pretty curtains, stylish furniture, and a sitting area for guests that is separate from the room in which the hospital bed is located.

As you might imagine, rich patients will eagerly flock to the individual accommodations, air conditioning, and creature comforts of the A1+ and A1 wards. But even people who are only moderately well-off will likely opt for B1 wards just to get air-conditioning and share a room with only three other patients.

With the richer people self-selecting into the more expensive ward classes, the large, unair-conditioned B2 and C wards are filled almost entirely with poorer patients.[1] The resulting separation between rich and poor based on ward class was, historically, so engrained that the Ministry of Health felt comfortable using it as the basis for distributing direct subsidies. For many years, direct subsidies flowed to anybody staying in B2 and C wards.

In recent years, though, the Ministry of Health has added means testing to its list of criteria for receiving direct subsidies. Higher earners are now excluded entirely from receiving direct subsidies, even if they stay in B2 and C wards. Means testing also allows the size of the direct subsidy flowing to a particular patient to be adjusted according to need, with the poorest patients receiving direct subsidies of up to 80 percent.

If a poorer patient wants a direct subsidy, though, he must use the money for his actual care, not for staying in a nicer ward. So highly subsidized patients *must* stay in the B2 and C class wards, which are consequently known as subsidized wards.

The better-off are also prevented from freeloading because anybody using a public hospital for inpatient cosmetic surgery is required to book themselves into either an A1+ or A1 ward. The same holds true for anybody looking to stay overnight at a public hospital while being treated by a visiting consultant (rather than by one of the public hospital's own staff physicians). Since it is only richer people who employ visiting consultants, anybody using visiting consultants has to stay in (and pay for!) an A1+ or A1 ward.

That enables a largely *voluntary* redistribution of wealth from the rich to the poor. Not only are the rich prevented from accessing direct subsidies, they are incentivized to voluntarily pay more for their inpatient visits than the poor. Because the additional money that they pay to stay in nicer rooms massively exceeds the cost of providing those nicer rooms, the rich patients' decision to opt for nicer lodgings generates a substantial surplus that can be recycled back toward the poor. Indeed, the only reason the per-night charges in C and B2 wards are so low is because richer people pay so much for the fancier wards.

A good analogy is the first-class section of an airplane. Whenever I fly from LA to New York, I purchase an economy seat. As a result, I have to pass the first-class passengers as I board the plane. They get big leather seats, wide arm rests, unlimited snacks, real silverware, much better food, and an open bar. But their first-class round-trip tickets will cost them upwards of $5,000. By contrast, my economy-class round-trip ticket will cost me only about $500. My ticket costs so much less partly because the airline is making so much profit off of the first-class passengers that it can lower the prices of economy class seats as it competes with other airlines for economy-class customers. Without those first-class passengers paying through the nose, the cost of economy-class tickets would have to go up.

Singapore understands this and has, like the airlines, found a way to get the rich to voluntarily overpay. When they do, the extra money can be transferred back toward the poor. Think Robin Hood, except that the rich are happy to be robbed. It's a nice trick.

Please note, though, that the trick is only possible because Singaporeans are not obsessed with trying to treat everybody exactly the same. By contrast, many Americans recoil at the thought of rich people staying in one-bed hospital suites with free Wi-Fi while poor patients are staying nine-to-a-room in unair-conditioned wards without televisions or telephones. It's as though we assume that the only fair way to run the world is to have everybody flying first-class and getting all the creature comforts of first class. Thus, you hardly ever see more than two beds to a room in a US hospital. And, in fact, most rooms are now single rooms with just one bed—and a private bathroom, and a TV, and a telephone, and air-conditioning, and Wi-Fi.

Singapore's Ministry of Health finds that fatuous. A healthcare system's purpose is to deliver healthcare, not hotel amenities. Singapore sees no problem at all with offering both economy and first-class wards. The truly needy can get top-quality healthcare in C wards without having to pay for fancy amenities. Even better, the rich who voluntarily pay for the perks of A1+ and A1 wards *overpay* for those perks, thereby allowing the government to shift that overspending back toward the poor. Under this system, the rich and the poor have equal access to top-quality healthcare—but the rich pay much more for it.

In my opinion, that seems much more "fair" than trying to give everyone a private room and free Wi-Fi. After all, what really matters is what Singapore delivers: high-quality care for all patients, regardless of their ability to pay.

Chapter 18

Pharmaceuticals
in Singapore

Because prescription drugs can cost so much in the United States,
I'm often asked how Singapore handles pharmaceuticals. Here's
the answer.

Singapore's Ministry of Health (MOH) uses competition
between generic and name-brand drugs, as well as between various
pharmaceutical companies, to keep prices down for everyone. Then,
on top of that, the MOH has put in place a subsidy system which
ensures that the poor will have access to essential medications,
regardless of cost.

The overall system is market-based. Once a drug is approved
for safety, market forces are allowed to determine which drugs get
used and which don't. In addition, the government allows drug
prices to be determined by supply and demand. If anyone needs help
paying for a prescription, he receives one or more subsidies that
reduce his share of the market price.

Pharmaceutical companies that want to sell a drug in Singapore
must first seek approval from the Health Sciences Authority (HSA),

which is part of the Ministry of Health. Interestingly, the HSA will typically license *any* drug that has already been approved by any of the major foreign drug-regulatory agencies (e.g., the European Medicines Agency, the US Food and Drug Administration, Australia's Therapeutic Goods Administration, Health Canada, or Japan's Pharmaceuticals and Medical Devices Agency).

The HSA does not require pharmaceutical companies to prove efficacy. They only have to prove safety. Any drug determined to be safe is put on the market, where consumers and physicians determine if it succeeds or not. Drugs in Singapore succeed or fail based on whether or not they can consistently attract paying customers, after doctors and patients have given the product a try and word of mouth about its effectiveness has spread.

Contrast this market-based approach with the "efficacy requirement" that the US Food and Drug Administration has enforced since 1962. Under the efficacy requirement, the FDA goes beyond the safety requirement by demanding that drugs also be proven to work as advertised. Demanding efficacy in addition to safety may sound like a good idea, but the higher standard imposed by that requirement has been a primary driver of the high cost of new drugs because it takes many years of massive, double-blind, randomized trials to prove efficacy. Estimates show that it now takes over a billion dollars and ten years of clinical trials to get a single drug through the approval process and on the market. The vast majority of those costs would disappear if we reverted to the pre-1962 "safety requirement," because it costs much less to prove safety alone as opposed to safety *plus* efficacy.

More importantly, we have scant evidence that the efficacy requirement did the public much good. As economist Sam Peltzman noted, the "market was very quickly weeding out ineffective drugs prior to 1962. Their sales decreased rapidly within a few months of introduction, and there was thus little room for the regulation to improve on market forces."[1] I believe that we should be like Singapore, or like our pre-1962 selves, and rely on the market to determine which drugs succeed or fail. We should keep the safety requirement, and then we should allow market forces to sort out efficacy at low cost by simply allowing doctors and patients to choose where to spend their limited budgets. Drugs that don't work won't survive.

Once a drug is on the market in Singapore, supply and demand determine its market price. But drug companies don't like supply and demand interacting freely because free-market competition tends to erode or even eliminate their profits. They would prefer to manipulate the market in order to increase their profits. In particular, they will aim for low supply coupled with high demand, as that combination will drive up selling prices without affecting production costs.

The most effective way for a drug company to limit supply is to rig the regulatory process so that only its own drugs get approved, while those of rival firms get denied. But as we've just gone over, Singapore's wide-open process for approving drugs makes this tactic impossible.

On the other hand, demand is still in play. One way for a drug company to try to increase the demand for its products is through advertising. In Singapore, it is perfectly legal for drug companies to take this approach. They are free to advertise both to the public as well as to medical doctors. Advertising is costly, however, and any advertising money spent by one firm will likely be countered by other firms. So there is little likelihood that any one firm will be able to use advertising to substantially or permanently increase the demand for its products relative to those of its rivals.

At the same time, competitive advertising between rival firms alerts the public to different drug options, which is very important. Once a patient learns about the existence of different drug options, she often starts to ask which one is the least expensive. So drug advertising leads to bargain shopping, which leads to drug makers competing on pricing.

If there were no government drug subsides in Singapore, that would be the end of the story. Unsubsidized supply and demand would determine the market prices of pharmaceuticals. But because the government *does* subsidize indigent patients, the drug companies have yet another possible way to increase demand. They can try to get purchases of their own drugs subsidized, knowing full well that whenever consumers face artificially low out-of-pocket costs, demand increases.

The government forestalls such increases in demand with an extremely clever drug-subsidy program which uses generic drugs, tiered subsidies, MediSave withdrawal limits, and deliberate obfuscation to prevent drug companies from being able to manipulate the subsidy system to drive up demand and increase their own profits.

As background, please note that about two-thirds of the 7,500 or so registered drugs in Singapore are inexpensive generics that put severe downward pressure on the market prices of brand-name drugs. When it comes time to distribute pharmaceutical subsidies, the overall list of 7,500 or so registered drugs is divvied up into three groups: the Standard Drug List, the Medication Assistance Fund Plus drug list, and the list of Non-Standard Drugs, which contains everything else. These three drug lists guide the MOH's three main drug-subsidy programs:

- The Standard Drug List, or SDL, consists of drugs that have been assessed to be both cost-effective and essential to the provision of medical care in Singapore. The SDL drugs are placed into one of two subcategories: SDL I and SDL II. The drugs on the SDL I list cost subsidized (i.e., indigent) patients only $1.40 per week, no matter how expensive their free-market price is. The drugs that are on the SDL II list are delivered to subsidized patients at a 50 percent subsidy relative to the market price.

- The Medication Assistance Fund Plus, or MAF+, helps patients pay for expensive drugs that have been assessed to be clinically necessary to treat certain conditions. Depending on a patient's financial need, MAF+ subsidizes up to 75 percent of the market price of these drugs.

- The Inpatient Drug Subsidy, or IDS, is a grant scheme similar to MediFund in which the government gives money to each public hospital to help inpatients pay for costly Non-Standard Drugs. A local medical committee at each hospital decides how the funds are allocated.

In addition to these three main drug-subsidy programs, the Community Health Assist Scheme (CHAS), which provides lower- and middle-income households with subsidies for outpatient medical and dental care at private clinics, also contains drug subsidies. That is especially useful because CHAS covers fifteen chronic conditions, which often require long-term adherence to a drug treatment regime. Thus, CHAS provides drug subsidies for long-term conditions including diabetes, hypertension, asthma, major depression, schizophrenia, lipid disorders, Parkinson's disease, and strokes.

To help prevent any of its drug-subsidy programs from raising drug prices, the MOH makes sure that many low-price generics are included on the SDL. Thus, a generic option is usually available when a doctor and patient have to choose which drug they should use to treat a particular condition. But even when a generic isn't available, the SDL and MAF+ subsidies by themselves cover up to 90 percent of all medication prescriptions written at Singapore's public hospitals and clinics. The IDS and CHAS drug subsidies are available to help with the rest.

As you would expect, pharmaceutical executives want their drugs included on either the SDL or the MAF+ drug lists, so that the subsidy system might increase demand. The experience of former Minister of Health Khaw Boon Wan is typical: "Every time a top CEO comes to see me, we usually do not talk about other things. He would say, 'Please put my new drug onto your list.'"[2]

To stymie this sort of lobbying, the Ministry of Health does something wonderfully counterintuitive. It doesn't publish any information on how drugs are selected to be on either the SDL or MAF+ drug lists. The MOH is intentionally opaque because, if there *were* explicit rules to follow for a drug to be included, those rules would be subject to lobbying efforts to expand those rules or to make exceptions. With no rules made public, drug-company CEOs can only lobby in very general terms.

The MOH's deliberate obfuscation doesn't stop there. The MOH also refuses to publish separate lists for the SDL I, SDL II, and MAF+ drugs. Instead, it publishes a combined list that contains all of the SDL I, SDL II, and MAF+ drugs listed together alphabetically. There is no way to tell from that combined list which drugs get an SDL I subsidy (covering all but $1.40 per week), which get an SDL II subsidy (50 percent of the market price), and which get an MAF+ subsidy (up to 75 percent of the market price). By doing this, the MOH further hamstrings lobbying efforts, because nobody can tell for certain which drugs are receiving which subsidies.

The MOH also controls excessive demand by limiting how much per day people can withdraw from their MediSave Accounts to pay for drugs. This works because most people are much more willing to pay for a drug with their accumulated MediSave money rather than other sources of cash. The preference for using MediSave money means that a person will often opt for a low-price generic, which he can cover entirely with MediSave money, rather than a more expensive non-generic (the cost of which would exceed the daily withdrawal limit).

Additionally, the MOH does its best to make sure there is robust competition between retail pharmacies. The Pharmaceutical Society of Singapore publishes drug prices for common chronic diseases including asthma, diabetes, and hypertension. Consumers can look up both the lowest and the highest price per dose charged by pharmacies in Singapore. With that information in hand, chronic disease patients can easily tell whether their local pharmacy is offering them a good deal. If not, they can take their business elsewhere.

Chapter 19

The 3Ms Dominate Incentives, Not Payments

3 Ms are privately funded, which means:

- MediSave is funded by private savings;
- MediShield's premiums, deductibles, and copays are paid for with private money (much of it flowing from MediSave accounts); and
- MediFund uses interest from an endowment operating independently of the government to pay the healthcare bills of Singapore's indigent.

A little-understood fact is that although the privately funded 3Ms form the foundation for Singapore's healthcare-financing system, they account for only a small fraction of Singapore's total healthcare spending. To see just how small this fraction is, take a look at Table 19.1, which provides a breakdown of Singapore's annual healthcare expenditures for the years 2002–2013.

Table 19.1: Singapore's Total National Healthcare Expenditures (Millions of Singapore Dollars)

Year	Total	Government	Medisave	Medishield	Medifund	Other Private
2002	5,956	1,558	361	77	26	3,934
2003	6,500	2,070	328	77	34	3,991
2004	6,870	1,778	367	84	32	4,609
2005	7,301	1,843	398	88	39	4,933
2006	7,810	2,010	445	113	40	5,202
2007	8,829	2,283	517	137	50	5,842
2008	9,788	2,814	558	161	59	6,196
2009	10,999	3,735	601	215	64	6,384
2010	11,768	3,846	678	249	79	6,916
2011	12,553	4,077	722	282	91	7,381
2012	13,926	4,809	767	315	102	7,933
2013	15,596	5,959	798	335	130	8,374

Source: Singapore Ministry of Health.

Notes: Direct Subsidies for medical treatment constitute the large majority of government healthcare expenditures. Medisave, Medishield, and Medifund are private sources of healthcare spending. Other private expenditures consist of payments made by private health insurance (including Medishield Advantage plans and employer-sponsored insurance plans), other employer medical benefits, and cash payments (from sources other than Medisave balances) made by consumers.

Focus on the bottom row, which gives data for 2013. That year, 3M expenditures (MediSave expenditures plus MediShield expenditures plus MediFund expenditures) totaled S$1,260 million, or just 8 percent of Singapore's total national healthcare expenditures of S$15.6 billion. By comparison, government healthcare expenditures (mostly direct subsidies) comprised 38 percent of total national healthcare expenditures, or almost five times more than 3M spending. Other sources of private spending (besides the 3Ms) constituted the remaining 54 percent of national healthcare spending. These additional private sources included payments made by MediShield Advantage plans, employer-sponsored health-insurance plans, other employer health benefits, and cash payments made by consumers for everything from aspirin, to cosmetic surgery, to paying extra to stay in fancy A1+ wards in public hospitals.

Figure 19.1 is a pie chart that gives the percentage shares of the various categories of spending that comprised Singapore's total 2013 national healthcare expenditures. Observe how small 3M expenditures are relative to total spending.

Figure 19.1: Percentage Shares of the Components of Singapore's Total National Healthcare Expenditure, 2013

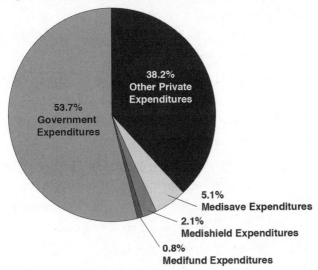

Source: Singapore Ministry of Health.

The 3Ms' small share of Singapore's overall healthcare spending has several important implications. First of all, the 3Ms' small share completely contradicts the misperception some people have that the 3Ms are Singapore's substitute for a national health service. Those people assume (incorrectly!) that *all* medical payments in Singapore are made under the 3Ms' structure of individual savings combined with high-deductible health insurance plus a safety net. But that's not the case. The 3Ms account for less than one-tenth of total healthcare spending, and they are dwarfed by both government healthcare spending and by other sources of private healthcare spending.

On the other hand, if you were to assess the 3Ms' small percentage naively, you might conclude that the 3Ms don't really matter that much. You might assume that you could do away with the 3Ms and still retain the low costs and high quality of Singapore's healthcare system.

Making that assumption would be a grave error. The 3Ms are the part of Singapore's healthcare system that actively promotes competition and prudence. As just one example, MediSave dollars give even the poor an incentive to shop around for the best deals and avoid wasteful spending, because any money they don't spend is theirs to keep. Because patients always have "skin in the game," they have an incentive to behave prudently and only consume when benefits exceed costs. Even better, their spending decisions force second parties to compete on both price and quality.

The degree to which those first-party spending decisions force second parties to compete can be fully appreciated only once you understand that *the spending decisions of first parties are amplified by third-party payments*. Why? Because the relatively small quantity of MediSave dollars spent by first parties directs a much larger amount of third-party spending in the same direction. Consider the following example. If Singapore General wants the government-funded subsidy money that will come from treating a poorer patient in a subsidized ward, it must first convince that patient to receive treatment at its *own* facility, rather than at any of the other public hospitals in Singapore. That patient may end up spending only a couple of hundred dollars of his own MediSave money, but his decision on where to get treated will bring with it a massive amount of additional subsidy revenue. His choice about where to spend his own money—a small amount though it may be—will determine where the substantial amount of third-party money will also go. In Singapore, the hospitals must compete for that third-party money.

So while the 3Ms themselves are small in volume, they are crucially important because they direct huge volumes of additional third-party spending. The huge total volume (3M spending plus the third-party spending that comes with it) forces second parties to compete intensely on price and quality, because the only way for them to receive *any* of the big third-party money is by pleasing first-party clients, rich or poor. As a result, the modest overall amount of 3M spending should be thought of as a small lever controlling a huge crane, a crane that dumps large piles of third-party money wherever the first parties choose.

Furthermore, the low prices that result from first-party comparison shopping are available to everyone, including third-party payers. So when the government uses direct subsidy money to pay for care for the poor, it pays the same low prices available to everyone, thanks to the 3Ms' ability to motivate and empower first-party decision makers.

Thus, while the 3Ms may appear diminutive when judged by their share of total expenditures, they are actually giants when viewed in terms of competition, efficiency, and downward price pressures. They give credence to the old proverb: "An ounce of prevention is worth a pound of cure." You don't need to make your entire healthcare system cash-and-carry to obtain the benefits of first-party payments and robust competition. An ounce of first-party spending is all that is needed for competition and prudence to yield a pound of efficiency benefits.

The 3Ms also provide for long-term financial solvency. While they account for just 8 percent of all healthcare spending in Singapore today, they could fund vastly more healthcare spending in the future. There is currently over S$80 billion sitting in Medisave accounts. That's enough money to run Singapore's entire healthcare system for over four years without having to obtain even a single penny of funding from any other source, public or private.

That huge stockpile of savings also implies that Singapore's healthcare financing system is the only one in the world with sufficient reserves set aside to take care of the rapidly aging baby boomer generation. Like other developed countries, Singapore has a rapidly aging population. That is not a problem for Singapore's long-run healthcare financing situation, though, because Singapore can tap MediSave's massive reserves. Singapore's citizenry can look to the future with confidence, knowing that there is *already* money set aside to pay for their future healthcare needs.

That puts Singapore in a much better position than other countries, whose baby boomer health-spending commitments will either have to be broken or kept only by means of massive tax increases which will likely cause severe problems for economic growth and productivity. So, here again, don't be fooled. The relatively small volume of the 3Ms' current expenditures should not be misunderstood. Not only are the 3Ms an ounce of prevention against waste and inefficiency; they are also an ounce of prevention against broken government pledges and greying populations.

Chapter 20

MediShield Life and the Future of Singapore's Healthcare System

Singapore's government is prudent and cautious. It does not commit to new spending projects unless it has the means to pay. Only after the 3Ms had been financially successful for many years did Prime Minister Lee Hsien Loong feel comfortable, in 2013, announcing that the government was going to modify MediShield to mandate universal participation, provide for increased payouts, and allow for all preexisting conditions. The new system would go into effect in 2015 and would be called MediShield Life, because it would offer lifetime, cradle-to-grave coverage.

You will recall that participation in MediShield had always been optional. It was true that everyone was defaulted into the system—newborns when their births were registered, immigrants and local adults when they first started working and paying into the CPF. But everybody had the right to withdraw themselves from MediShield. Those signing the form for withdrawal were still required to contribute to MediSave, but they were free to go without MediShield.[1]

I happened to be visiting Singapore about a month before the prime minister made the announcement about MediShield Life at the 2013 National Independence Day celebrations. In talking with various government officials and health economists, it was clear that there had been political pressure over the previous few years to make MediShield compulsory, thereby transforming it into a mandatory, universal health insurance system. The political pressure was the result of two major complaints.

First, MediShield only offered coverage until people turned ninety-two. Anyone older had to pay for their own medical bills out of MediSave or, if that ran out, by relying on family members, charity, or MediFund. This seemed deeply impious in a Confucian society that revered the elderly. No one wanted anybody's great-grandmother to suddenly become unable to pay her medical bills.

Secondly, a person relying on private health insurance through an employer could lose that coverage if they got fired, laid off, or switched jobs. If they had previously opted out of MediShield, then those individuals could be caught without insurance coverage. The electorate did not like that. They wanted everyone to be covered at all times.

To that end, the prime minister announced that MediShield Life would be mandatory for citizens and permanent residents. Those enrolled at birth would have cradle-to-grave coverage; the elderly would be covered until they died; and nobody would ever accidentally end up without insurance if they became unemployed. Under MediShield Life, anybody who kept up with their premium payments would have insurance for life.

The next major change the prime minister announced regarded increased payouts. The annual deductible would stay the same, but the maximum copay rate would fall from 20 percent to 10 percent. Additionally, MediShield Life would have higher daily, annual, and lifetime claims limits. The daily ward charges limit would be raised from S$900 to $S1,200; the annual total claims limit would be raised from S$70,000 to S$100,000; and the lifetime claims limit would be raised from S$300,000 to infinity—that is, there would no longer be a lifetime claims limit at all. As you might imagine, these changes were big crowd pleasers.

The final change was for MediShield Life to guarantee coverage for any and all preexisting conditions. This change was made possible by MediShield Life's requirement that everybody participate. To see why this matters, you must understand how voluntary insurance systems such as MediShield tend to fail if they cover preexisting conditions. As an example, consider fire insurance. Imagine if people could wait until *after* their homes burned down to apply for fire insurance—that is, if they could wait until after their houses had developed a preexisting condition. If that were allowed, the insurer would not be able to collect enough in premiums to pay for all the houses that would eventually burn down because not enough people would be willing to pay premiums in advance.[2] The insurance system would collpase under a tsunami of adverse selection.

But when participation is made mandatory, that sort of free riding becomes impossible. When you require everyone to pay premiums in advance, you don't have to worry about the insurance company's ability to collect enough money ahead of time to pay for all the eventual claims. Making MediShield Life mandatory guarantees that enough premium monies will be collected in advance to pay out on all the future healthcare costs associated with preexisting conditions.

However, people entering a health insurance system with preexisting conditions will tend to have substantially higher future medical costs than those entering without preexisting conditions. This creates an issue of fairness: those with preexisting conditions will be taking more from the insurance pool than those without. With this in mind, is it really fair to charge both groups the same premium?

It might be, if you envisioned your insurance system as a lightly disguised welfare system, the purpose of which was the transfer of resources from one group to another. But Singapore's government doesn't want that; its commitment to promoting individual responsibility means it always wants to remind people that costs should not be cavalierly dumped on other people. This is especially true with preexisting conditions resulting from voluntary choices—things like alcoholism-induced liver cirrhosis or smoking-induced lung cancer.

With all this in mind, the government decided that while MediShield Life would cover preexisting conditions, it would charge higher premiums to reflect the reality that those with preexisting conditions will accrue higher future costs. To that end, MediShield Life charges a person with one or more preexisting conditions a 30 percent higher premium for the first ten years of coverage. After those ten years, he or she will be charged the same premium as anybody else in the same age bracket.

By implementing the 30 percent surcharge, MediShield Life will be able to collect enough additional money to cover the higher costs associated with preexisting conditions. As a result, MediShield Life can remain, at its heart, true insurance, rather than a wealth-transfer scheme. Its base premiums will reflect the costs and risks facing those without preexisting conditions, while the 30 percent premium will reflect the additional costs facing those with preexisting conditions.

That being said, it *is* expensive to increase payouts, provide universal coverage, and include the elderly. Premiums therefore had to increase. Yet, by American standards, Singapore's premiums remain *wondrously low.*

The most expensive annual premium is S$1,530 per year for elderly people over ninety years of age living in households with incomes in excess of S$2,600 per month. Every other premium is less, either because the insured are younger or because their lower household income qualifies them for subsidized premiums.

The subsidies are significant. For elderly people over ninety living in households with monthly incomes of S$1,100 or less, the annual subsidized premium is just S$765, or about half of the S$1,530 unsubsidized premium. As another example, the unsubsidized premium for forty-two-year-olds is S$435 per year, whereas a person of the same age who lives in a household with a monthly income of less than S$1,100 only has to pay S$305 per year. And for those twenty and younger, the MediShield Life premium is S$130 per year for those living in households with monthly incomes of S$2,600 or more, but only S$98 per year for those living in households with monthly incomes of S$1,100 or less.

To give you a sense of how much higher MediShield Life premiums are relative to MediShield premiums, let me compare some MediShield premiums (which were the same for all income groups) with *unsubsidized* MediShield Life premiums (which only apply to the well-off). That comparison will give you a sense of the maximum possible amounts by which premiums jumped from MediShield to MediShield Life.

For those twenty years old or younger, the MediShield premium was S$50 per year, whereas the unsubsidized MediShield Life premium is S$130 per year. For people in their forties, the MediShield premium was S$220 per year, whereas the unsubsidized MediShield Life premium is S$435 pear year. For people in their late sixties, the MediShield premium was S$540 per year, compared with an unsubsidized MediShield Life premium of S$815. And for those in their late eighties, the premiums went up from S$1,190 with MediShield to S$1,500 with unsubsidized MediShield Life.

I should also mention that, in addition to the income-based subsidies for the less affluent, the government also added an additional set of subsidies for the country's older cohorts. As discussed in Chapter 16, many older Singaporeans were already almost finished with their working lives when MediSave was established in 1985. As a result, many of them had only small balances in their MediSave Accounts upon retirement. To help them, the government is subsidizing their MediShield Life premiums, as well as using general tax revenues to make annual bonus contributions (colloquially referred to as "top offs") to their MediSave Accounts. Between the premium subsidies and the top offs, MediShield Life will be essentially free for Singapore's oldest citizens.

As you consider how generous the government is being with MediShield Life, please note that this generosity is only possible because of the financial stability of MediShield and the overall 3M system. Singapore can be so generous only because it has been so efficient for so long. With its finances in great shape, Singapore is free to invest in the health and wellbeing of its citizens.

We, sadly, are not in that position. Our healthcare system has massive, unfunded public liabilities and hardly any private money set aside for future health expenses. But as I will explain in the next few chapters, much has already been done in the United States to prove that Singapore-style healthcare reform dramatically reduces medical spending. The declines are so large that, if the reforms were to be implemented nationwide, they would instantly flip Medicaid and Medicare from insolvency to solvency while also causing individuals to amass huge amounts of money in their health savings accounts.

So don't be too pessimistic. Just because we've screwed things up thus far doesn't mean we can't turn it all around. As German Chancellor Bismarck is said to have remarked over a hundred years ago, "God has a special providence for fools, drunks, and the United States of America."

Chapter 21

The State of Indiana's Consumer-Driven Healthcare Plan

Thus far, I've shown you that Singapore has the most effective, least costly healthcare system of any developed nation. I've also shown you how they do it.

The question for America then becomes: Can we *really* copy Singapore? Can what they do over there *possibly* work over here?

The answer is a resounding "Yes!" not just in theory, but in practice. We have domestic examples of Singapore-style healthcare systems working wonders right here in the United States.

UNDERSTANDING CONSUMER-DRIVEN HEALTHCARE PLANS

Our local versions of Singapore-style healthcare plans are known as consumer-driven healthcare plans, or CDHPs. CDHPs always contain two elements: a health savings account (like MediSave) and a high-deductible health insurance plan (like MediShield).[1] The two are intended to work seamlessly in tandem, with the accumulated balances in health savings accounts paying for the deductibles and copays of the high-deductible health insurance plan.

The high deductibles and substantial copays are, of course, intentional. As you know from reading earlier chapters, these forms of cost sharing incentivize consumers to shop around for the best combination of price and quality—hence the designation "consumer-driven." But because participants are not legally required to actually put savings into their health-savings accounts, many CDHP participants have found their accounts under-funded relative to the amount of cost sharing with which they are subsequently confronted. Keep this in mind as we discuss CDHPs. There is a need to ensure that they are backed by sufficiently funded health-savings accounts—either through mandatory savings, generous contributions by plan sponsors, or government grants for the poor and elderly.

In 2018, 29 percent of American workers were enrolled in CDHPs.[2] The other 71 percent were enrolled in either preferred-provider organizations (PPOs), health-maintenance organizations (HMOs), point-of-service (POS) plans, or indemnity plans. PPOs enrolled 49 percent, HMOs enrolled 16 percent, POS plans enrolled 6 percent, and indemnity plans enrolled less than 1 percent.[3]

Collectively, CDHPs save a lot of money in premium costs. In 2018, the average CDHP premium for single coverage was $6,459.[4] That was about 8 percent less than the average premium for single coverage in an HMO ($6,969) and about 10 percent less than the average premium for single coverage in a PPO ($7,149). With respect to family coverage, the average premium for a CDHP in 2018 was $18,602, or about 4 percent less than the average premium for family coverage in an HMO ($19,445) and about 8 percent less than the average premium for family coverage in a PPO ($20,324).

As you would expect after learning about MediShield, CDHPs have lower premiums because the high-deductibles and substantial copays encourage prudence. As I show below, however, lower premiums are only the tip of the iceberg when it comes to the money that CDHPs can save. The real action is in how they change consumer behavior in ways that lead to massive decreases in consumption without any decreases in health outcomes.

CONSUMER-DRIVEN HEALTHCARE PLANS CHANGE BEHAVIOR

Ninety-one percent of CDHPs have first-dollar coverage for preventive care, which does encourage participants to spend freely on prevention. As a result, it's not surprising that a study by Aetna Insurance of 2.3 million people enrolled in its various healthcare plans found that CDHP participants were more engaged in their healthcare than individuals enrolled in traditional plans.[5] The CDHP participants went in for more prostate, cervical and colorectal cancer screenings. They went in for more mammograms and had more immunizations. They were twice as likely to use online health tools such as symptom checkers, online fitness logs, and computerized health assessments.

All that engagement appears to have paid off nicely in terms of treatment continuity, as the study found that CDHP participants were 30 percent less likely to have gaps in care. Along the same lines, a study by the Employee Benefit Research Institute found that CDHP participants were more likely to access health-risk assessments and health-promotion programs.[6]

It is, however, the high-deductible on non-preventive care that generates CDHPs' big cost advantage.[7] The high deductible incentivizes participants to shop around, which involves seeking out information from third-party sources rather than simply trusting your insurance company to steer you in the right direction. Thus, the

Employee Benefit Research Institute found that CDHP participants were almost a third more likely to seek information on provider cost and quality from sources other than their own health plan.

A study by the American Academy of Actuaries shows that CDHP participants save money in two ways: by using fewer inpatient services and by spending less on emergency room visits and acute care services. The reductions in spending also extend to pharmaceuticals. When both generic drugs and chemically identical name-brand drugs are available, CDHP participants opt for generic drugs at a much higher rate than do people in traditional health insurance plans. This saves major costs without reducing the quality of care.

CDHP plans also include chronic care. Participants with chronic conditions in CDHP plans receive recommended care at comparable or higher rates than people enrolled in traditional plans. Patients suffering from chronic conditions such as high blood pressure, high cholesterol levels, and congestive heart failure also have medication-adherence rates as high as those of participants in traditional health insurance plans. Patients with CDHP plans also use up to 23 percent more preventive services than do chronically ill patients with traditional insurance.

The high participation rates for preventive care and chronic care found among CDHP participants are very important because they argue against the impression that some people have that CDHPs will create really bad health and behavioral incentives. In particular, some skeptics assume that CDHP participants will become too reluctant to spend out of their health savings accounts; they fear that participants will be so eager to conserve their savings that they will skip out on annual exams, mammograms, and preventive screening tests.

The actual data that we just reviewed argues strongly against those worries. But while the results cited above can go a long way toward allaying the skeptics' fears, they do not by themselves offer unassailable evidence about the behavioral effects of CDHPs with respect to preventive care. There are two problems: the first is that we do not have evidence about how an individual's health-spending behavior changes when he enters a CDHP. Does it improve or worsen? Since we didn't follow the behavior of individuals before and after, we just don't know.

The second problem is that people were not assigned to CDHPs at random. They volunteered. As a result, we have no idea as to whether the lower spending demonstrated by CDHP participants was the result of the incentive effects of CDHPs, or because a certain type of person chose the CDHP option. For instance, perhaps only healthier or better-educated or more financially astute people chose CDHPs. If so, we wouldn't really be able to say anything about how entering a CDHP might affect somebody sicker, or not so well-educated, or less financially astute. Without a randomized participant pool, we can't know if the results we see above are an accurate representation of the population as a whole.

A/B TESTING CONSUMER-DRIVEN HEALTHCARE PLANS

The remainder of this chapter reviews the extremely strong evidence that speaks to the first problem—that we normally don't know what individuals' health situations are like before and after switching to CDHPs. Although that's true, it is also true that in cases where there *is* before-and-after evidence for individuals, we see that CDHPs massively cut spending without hurting health outcomes. Between this chapter and the next, we will go over evidence that indicates that, if we were to enroll everyone in the country in a Singapore-style CDHP, we would be able to save *everyone* lots of money without hurting their health outcomes.

Let's begin with the before-and-after evidence on individuals entering CDHPs. In 2007, the state of Indiana started offering a Singapore-style health insurance option—that is, a CDHP—to state employees in addition to the traditional types of health insurance such as HMOs, PPOs, etc., that employees had been offered every year up to that point.

As you would expect, the Singapore-style plan combined high-deductible health insurance with health savings. The insurance portion had an annual deductible of $2,750, while the savings portion utilized health savings accounts, or HSAs. Congress created HSAs in 2002 to let people save for future health expenditures, tax-free.[8] They were designed to be used in conjunction with high-deductible health insurance plans, so HSAs initially found their greatest popularity among the self-employed, because high-deductible health insurance plans are substantially less expensive than traditional, low-deductible health insurance plans—especially when you have to purchase insurance on your own rather than getting it as part of group coverage through an employer.[9]

During the 2000s, however, more and more firms began offering HSAs to their employees. As a result, 29 percent of American workers with employer-sponsored health insurance currently have CDHPs. That's a very good thing, because before-and-after evidence shows that these plans massively reduce healthcare expenditures without making people "pennywise but pound foolish" about preventive care.

How do we know this? A study ordered by Mitch Daniels, the governor of Indiana back in 2007, shows us the data. Governor Daniels had previously been the CEO of pharmaceutical giant Eli Lilly as well as the director of the Office of Management and Budget for the federal government. He's a numbers guy. He went out and hired a consulting company to look through the healthcare-utilization data generated by the state's employees.

What the consultants found was startling. Employees who switched from one of the traditional health insurance plans to the Singapore-style plan reduced their spending by 35 percent. Yes, *35 percent.*

Remember, we are talking about person-by-person comparisons here. Consider a state of Indiana employee named Tommy. In every previous year, Tommy was in a traditional plan. Then he switches to a Singapore-style plan. He is the same guy, with the same behavioral tendencies, the same level of education, and the same preexisting conditions... but his spending falls 35 percent. Nothing changed about him. The massive decrease in spending can only be attributed to behavioral changes—not to CDHPs having a tendency to attract healthier participants.

The consultants analyzed the state's data to identify what behaviors changed.[10] They found that state workers who switched to the Singapore-style CDHP:

- Visited emergency rooms and physicians 67 percent less often;
- Were admitted to hospitals half as often; and
- Opted for generic drugs rather than brand-name equivalents so much more often that the average cost of filling a prescription decreased by eighteen dollars.

More importantly, the state employees who enrolled in the Singapore-style CDHP showed no evidence of deferring needed care or going in any less often for preventive measures like routine physicals or mammograms.

Thus, there were no problems with people becoming "pennywise but pound foolish." Because participants kept going in for preventive care as often as they had when they were on traditional, low-deductible insurance, we can be quite confident that the 35 percent spending reduction is permanent. We don't have to worry about a situation in which current spending goes down due to neglect only to rise precipitously in the future (which can occur whenever current neglect leads to severe future health problems). With preventive-care utilization unchanged, future health expenses should also be unchanged.

So what drives the behavioral changes that end up reducing healthcare expenditures by 35 percent? For the most part, it's the high deductible. When people are paying the first $2,750 entirely out of pocket, they think twice about when and why they will go to the emergency room, visit an urgent care center, or see a physician.

By contrast, if your health insurance is of the low-deductible variety or has only a very low required payment for office visits, you will likely go in any time your kid has the sniffles, any time your knee feels slightly weird after playing softball, and so on. With an artificially low cost, you will go see the doctor much more often.

The same is true with hospital admissions. To see why, consider concussions. When I was a kid, doctors would just shine a pen light in your eyes to see if they were still contracting and dilating properly. After that, they would almost always send you home. But these days, hospitals know that if a patient has traditional health insurance, they can charge the insurance company a boatload of money—at least a couple of thousand dollars—if you are admitted overnight "for observation." They *want* to admit you.

But if you are on a high-deductible plan, the hospital won't be charging the insurance company. They will be charging you. So naturally, you will consider the invitation very carefully. And in many cases, you're likely to decide against it. Hence the 50 percent fall in hospital admissions among the state of Indiana employees who switched to the high-deductible plan.

Finally, consider those employees' higher propensity to select generic drugs. Generic drugs are chemically equivalent to name-brand drugs. To opt for an expensive name-brand drug instead of a generic one is simply throwing away money. Unfortunately, people on normal insurance plans do that a lot, mostly because they don't have to pay very much for their medications under those plans.

By contrast, people paying for their own prescriptions tend to opt for generics whenever they are available. In Indiana, the rate at which state employees opted for brand-name drugs when generics were available fell from 93 percent to just 13 percent after they entered the high-deductible plan and had to pay for all medication expenses below the deductible.

That massive reduction in brand-name drug usage demonstrates that when people are responsible for paying for their own medicines, they are happy to go generic. It's only when someone else is picking up all or most of the tab that they favor brand-name pharmaceuticals. That behavior is like a person who only orders wine at dinner when they can bill an expense account; when they have to spend their own money, they're happy to go without.

INSPIRING PRUDENCE—AFFORDABLY

The Indiana CDHP is very affordable for employees. Each year, the state does two things for employees who select the Singapore-style plan for themselves and their families. First, the state pays the full premium for a family policy that has a $2,750 annual deductible. Then, it deposits $2,750 into the employee's HSA as a gift. By doing so, the employee automatically has enough cash on hand to pay that year's deductible.

Next, for any spending between $2,750 and $8,000 per year, there's a 20 percent copay, meaning that the employee has to pay 20 percent of any spending between $2,750 per year and $8,000 per year.[11] If spending exceeds $8,000 per year, all further expenses are 100 percent paid for by the insurance company.

If you calculate what 20 percent of the gap between $2,750 and $8,000 is, you will find that it amounts to only $1,050. So the absolute worst-case scenario for an employee is spending $1,050 per year (beyond the $2,750 that was gifted into their HSAs) on healthcare. That's not bad at all, especially in the context of family policies and coverage for any number of dependents.

But it gets even better.

Imagine that, in Year 1, you don't spend all of the $2,750 in your HSA. Suppose you only spend $1,500. The remaining $1,250 would remain in your HSA account and be available to you the next year. That $1,250 would be added to the $2,750 HSA deposit you would receive for Year 2. Your initial balance at the start of the second year would be $4,000.

As a result, you wouldn't have to spend any money out of pocket at all during the second year, even if you were hit with massive medical bills. For instance, suppose you ran up $85,000 due to a severe car accident. Well, as we established, the first $2,750 would be on you, with an additional $1,050 to cover 20 percent of the gap between $2,750 and $8,000. Well, guess what? You have all that money in your HSA. You've got the $2,750 for the deductible because you were given that much money in Year 2, and you've got the $1,050 for the copay, because you retained $1,250 from the previous year. Thanks to having $4,000 at the start of Year 2, all your medical spending for the second year comes out of your HSA.

Generalizing from this example, you can see that with even a modest amount of saving in the first few years, a person could easily save up enough in their HSA that, even if they had several bad years in a row, they would never have to spend any money from personal savings or other sources of income or wealth on healthcare.

Even better is the fact that the insurance company covers everything over $8,000. This means that there is zero chance that a healthcare catastrophe could ever financially wipe out a family. With $1,050 per year in non-HSA medical spending being the absolute worst-case scenario, bankruptcy is not an issue. If a medical disaster strikes, families can focus on what really matters: healing.

Indiana's Singapore-style CDHP was a huge hit with state employees. The first year it was offered, only 2 percent of them switched over from the traditional options that had always been available. But through simple word of mouth, fully 70 percent of state employees switched into the plan the second year. They loved the security that came from seeing their HSA balances growing. Each additional dollar brought peace of mind.

By law, HSAs are portable. Workers know they can switch employers and still keep the money in their accounts, continuing to provide security for their families. Even better, HSA balances grow tax-free. And because the accounts are personal property, any unspent balances can be willed to heirs upon death. This provides more security for people's families, even after they're gone.

As we close out this chapter, let me emphasize that the state of Indiana's before-and-after comparisons demonstrate unequivocally that participating in a CDHP changes behavior among the employees who chose to enroll. The question then becomes: how would everybody else react? Would all the other people—the ones who did not opt for the CDHP—also cut spending massively if they were enrolled in a CDHP?

There's only one way to answer that question. We need randomized sample groups to prevent different types of people from self-selecting into different plans. We need randomization to be able to isolate the effect of the plans from the type of people entering the plans.

In Chapter 22, I'll show you the results of two randomized health insurance experiments. These experiments demonstrate that, even when people are enrolled into different types of health plans completely randomly, individuals in a Singapore-style plan spend less while remaining just as healthy.

Chapter 22

RAND and Oregon: Slashing Spending without Hurting Health

T hus far in US history, only two large-scale, fully randomized studies have examined how people behave under different health insurance schemes. The first was conducted back in the 1970s and '80s by the RAND Corporation, a major think tank. The second is currently underway in Oregon.

The RAND study collected field data from November 1974 to January 1982. It was funded with a $50 million grant from the federal government's Department of Health, Education, and Welfare (now known as the Department of Health and Human Services). The study recruited 2,750 families, which together contained 7,691 individuals. To provide geographic diversity, the families were selected from six cities across America, some urban, some rural.[1] Each family was randomized into participating for either three or five years. Only people younger than sixty-one were enrolled, so that their three-to-five-year participation in the program would be finished before any of them turned sixty-five and could go on Medicare.

Each family was also randomly assigned to one of six types of health insurance plans, created specifically for the experiment. One was an HMO-style medical cooperative. Anyone assigned to that plan received healthcare totally free of charge. The second was a health insurance plan that had one premium per family but separate deductibles for each family member. What we are interested in, however, are the other four plans, which combined high deductibles with copays, like Singapore's MediShield and the CDHP plan that Indiana offers to state employees. A total of 3,958 individuals from 2,005 families were enrolled into these four Singapore-style plans.

Under all four of these plans, the annual deductible was set at $1,000 per year, unless a family was poor. For poor families, the deductible was set at either 5, 10, or 15 percent of household income, depending on how poor the family was. In all cases, the insurance policy covered all spending above each family's deductible.

As an additional control, any family that had been assigned to a plan that was less generous than their previous insurance policy was paid an amount sufficient to prevent them from becoming financially worse off. That amount was equal to their highest possible loss and was paid in installments every four weeks, *irrespective of their use of medical services*. In this way, RAND preemptively controlled for any changes in behavior that could be ascribed to a family feeling impoverished relative to their old insurance policy. With that control in place, their behavior during the experiment could be ascribed to the different incentives put in place by the different copay rates, rather than to the participants changing their medical spending behavior because they felt impoverished by the plan into which they had been randomized.

The four insurance policies had identical, comprehensive coverage which included physician, hospital, dental, vision, hearing, and mental health services. Also included were prescription drug coverage, chiropractors, audiologists, clinical psychologists (with up to fifty-two mental health visits covered per year), optometrists, physical therapists, and speech therapists.

What differed was the copay rates for the four plans. They were set, respectively, at 0 percent, 25 percent, 50 percent, and 95 percent. There are two things we must note: first, the people randomized into the 0 percent copay rate were essentially guaranteed unlimited free healthcare. They would pay nothing on all spending up to their deductible and then zero percent on any spending above the deductible.

Secondly, the families randomized into the 95 percent copay rate were given financial incentives similar to those encountered by Singapore's MediShield participants and by the people participating in the state of Indiana plan. That's because those plans enforce a 100 percent copay rate until their respective annual deductibles are met.

In what follows, we are going to be most interested in comparing the group that gets unlimited free care due to their 0 percent copay with the group facing the 95 percent copay. Two questions are relevant: Will they differ in total healthcare expenditures? And will they show any differences in health outcomes?

RESULTS UNFOLD

To find out, participants were given comprehensive physical exams both before they started using their insurance and after they finished the program either three or five years later. By comparing the participants' health before and after, researchers could ascertain whether different plans led to different health outcomes.

The RAND study had two major results. First, the families randomized into paying 95 percent copays spent 30 percent less than the people randomized into unlimited free care with the 0 percent copay.

In this fully randomized study, we can see a spending reduction very similar to the 35 percent reduction observed when Indiana state employees self-selected into a CDHP plan. As a result, we can safely assume that the cost savings demonstrated by the state of Indiana was not due to sample-selection bias or a disproportionate enrollment of healthier people. The state of Indiana's CDHP lowers costs. Period.

The second big result of the RAND study was that health outcomes were statistically identical across all four plans. In particular, people with the 95 percent copay ended up just as healthy as the people getting unlimited free care. This implies that massively cutting back on health-care spending can be done without hurting health outcomes.

Of course, we already knew that in an international sense, because Singapore is getting the world's best health outcomes while spending 75 percent less than the United States and 50 to 60 percent less than Canada, the UK, and other developed countries. But it was neverthe-less reassuring to find out that the same held true *in America*. The RAND results eliminated the possibility that Singapore's ability to deliver high quality at low cost might have been due to things like genetics, diet, or culture. Because RAND randomized which partici-pants were in each group, we know that we, too, can cut healthcare spending massively without adversely affecting healthcare outcomes.

The only possible exception that the RAND study found was related to the subset of participants who were the most sickly upon enrollment. If you look just at that subset, the people randomized into the 95 percent copay group had worse outcomes on two health mea-sures—corrected visual acuity and risk of dying—as compared with the other members of that sickly subset who were randomized into unlimited free care with the 0 percent copay. Among the subset of participants who were the most sickly *and* the poorest upon enroll-ment, those randomized into the 95 percent copay group had worse health outcomes in two health measures—blood pressure and risk of dying—as compared with other members of the sickly and poor subset who were randomized into unlimited free care with no copays.

A few healthcare advocates have tried to seize on those results as evidence that high-deductible health insurance plans are dangerous for our most vulnerable citizens. But that contention is highly dubious at best; at worst, it's intentional misrepresentation.

To see why, note that the RAND Corporation kept track of thirty different health metrics, things like diastolic blood pressure and cholesterol levels. For twenty-seven of the thirty, participant outcomes were statistically indistinguishable, regardless of income level, initial health, or which group they had been randomized into. Twenty-seven out of thirty is 90 percent. So the general conclusion must be that *high-deductible health insurance plans do not hurt health outcomes, even for the poor and sickly.*

In addition, the difference in one of the three remaining health outcomes—corrected visual acuity—was so small that it would have had no effect whatsoever on patients' lives. Among the 25 percent of participants with the worst corrected vision (i.e., wearing glasses) at the start of the experiment, those randomized into the 0 percent copay group ended up with 20/24 corrected vision at the end of the experiment as compared with 20/25 vision for those randomized into any of the other three copay groups. As a glasses-wearer myself, I can testify that there is no noticeable difference between 20/24 vision and 20/25 vision. Thus, we can hardly take that difference in outcomes as any sort of proof that high-deductible health insurance hurts the most vulnerable. To say otherwise is blind demagoguery! (Pun intended.)

The results for blood pressure and the risk of dying are also statistically dubious. If you slice a large sample into enough subsamples, you are likely to find some subsamples where there *seems* to be an effect, but the difference that you see is actually just due to random chance. If a researcher opts for 10-percent "confidence intervals" when looking for effectiveness, then about 10 percent of the subsamples will show a "statistically significant effect" just out of random chance, when there is actually no causal effect. Given that more than three hundred academic papers have been written about the RAND study's results and so many authors have crunched the data over and over, it's not surprising that a few found subsamples in which there seemed to be differences between the parts of those subsamples randomized into the 0 percent copay group and the parts of those subsamples randomized into the 95 percent copay group. What really matters is that, *despite* slicing and dicing so much, researchers still couldn't find any statistically significant differences in the vast majority of subsamples they tried.

More importantly, they weren't able to find any statistically significant differences when they looked at the *entire sample*. For the sample as a whole, health outcomes were unaffected by spending rates or the amount of usage. Whether randomization led to higher or lower spending and usage, people were equally healthy.

That point is very important. Those on unlimited free care, thanks to the 0 percent copay, spent 37 percent more on physician services than those on the 25 percent copay and 67 percent more than those on the 95 percent copay.

But since we know everybody ended up equally healthy, those vast differences in usage demonstrate that consuming 37 percent or even 67 percent more of physician services *doesn't make people healthier*. We could put those people on high-deductible, Singapore-style plans and expect them to be just as healthy, even after the incentives of those plans cause them to cut back on usage.

LEARNING FROM OREGON

If you still have any doubts about whether high-deductible health insurance might hurt society's most vulnerable, I have great news for you. The state of Oregon inadvertently ended up running a fully randomized health insurance experiment that only involved individuals eligible for Medicaid—that is, people who, by definition, are poor. This experiment tests whether giving poor people Medicaid improves their health outcomes, as well as whether medical spending increases when you give people an insurance plan that covers all healthcare costs (as Medicaid does).

I describe the Oregon experiment as "inadvertent" because, in early 2008, the state of Oregon decided that it had just enough room in its annual budget to offer Medicaid health insurance coverage to an additional ten thousand people. Because demand was almost certainly going to exceed those ten thousand spots, the state held a lottery for the right to apply. For five weeks, anybody could register for the lottery by phone, fax, mail, the internet, or by signing up in person. In the end, 89,824 individuals registered. Of those, 35,169 were randomly selected to apply. Of that number, however, 60 percent didn't even bother turning in an application. And, of the remainder, only about half actually met the income test and other requirements needed to qualify for Medicaid. The ten thousand who were finally enrolled were those who first won the right to apply, then bothered to apply, and then met the requirements.

But because the right to apply was assigned randomly, the state of Oregon had inadvertently created a randomized experiment. Researchers could isolate the effect of receiving Medicaid by comparing the health outcomes of the ten thousand people who were enrolled (i.e. those who both won the right to apply *and* met the requirements) with those of two other groups: those who won the lottery but didn't meet the requirements, and those who signed up for the lottery but didn't win.[2] As a result, we have a randomized experiment that can answer two very important questions about Medicaid: Does enrolling poor people into Medicaid improve health outcomes? And does enrolling poor people into Medicaid affect medical spending?

The answer to the first question was published in the *New England Journal of Medicine*. Being randomized into Medicaid "generated no [statistically] significant improvement in measured physical health outcomes," including death, diabetes, high cholesterol, and high blood pressure.[3]

The only area that improved enough to be considered statistically significant was enrollees' self-reports of their own rates of depression and feelings of financial security. Several pundits latched onto the self-reported results about depression and called them "proof" that putting people on Medicaid was a good thing. After all, the self-reported rates of depression were 9 percentage points lower (30 percent vs. 21 percent). Unfortunately for those pundits, the self-reports were made after the ten thousand were enrolled *but before they started receiving any benefits*. That means that the improvement in the self-reported rate of depression was either a placebo effect or simply part of the warm glow that the recipients understandably received from a greater sense of security. As you would expect, having health insurance made people *feel* better. But as for actually *being* better, the enrollees did no better than the controls on the health variables measured by researchers.

Crucially, this warm-glow effect would almost certainly be achieved by any Singapore-style healthcare system that enrolled the poor. There is no reason to laud Medicaid in particular for giving people a greater sense of security. Any system promising affordable healthcare would do the same. I, of course, favor a Singapore-style solution because it would not only give poor people a warm glow with its promises, but would *actually fulfill those promises* by delivering high quality care at extremely low costs.

By contrast, healthcare usage and spending in the Oregon experiment went way up for the ten thousand enrolled in Medicaid. Being enrolled increased hospital admissions by 30 percent, outpatient care by 35 percent,[4] and emergency room visits by 40 percent.[5]

So it comes as no surprise that spending was 36 percent higher among those randomized into Medicaid. Thus, we see that while spending and usage went way up, there was no measurable improvement in health outcomes. Given what we know from the state of Indiana and the RAND health insurance experiment, this combination of effects is not surprising. Unlimited free care massively increases usage without improving healthcare outcomes, meaning you can massively cut back on medical spending without adversely affecting healthcare outcomes.

Please note that these are the results of a fully randomized experiment that eliminates the possibility of self-selection bias. Thanks to randomization, we know that the massive differences in spending and usage that we see across the various groups are due to differences in the health-insurance plans, rather than to the members of those groups differing from each other in initial health status or other measures. Thus, we have eliminated the second caveat that I brought up with respect to the state of Indiana's results. Even in a fully randomized study, high-deductible health insurance causes people to massively cut back on their health expenditures without hurting their health. Therefore, we can be confident that if we implemented Singapore-style health reform all across America, it would have the same beneficial results that we observed in Indiana.

THE NUTS AND BOLTS OF REDUCING COSTS

A final point should be made. The state of Indiana achieved a 35 percent decrease in spending, but RAND found only a 30 percent decrease. Does that mean that randomization reduced the amount of cost savings?

A variety of factors suggest otherwise.

To begin with, the RAND study's financial incentives were not as strong as those implemented by the state of Indiana. As just one example, the highest copay group in the RAND study had to pay 95 percent of all medical spending below the deductible. By contrast, Indiana participants had to pay 100 percent of all spending below the deductible. That 5 percent difference may not seem like much, but it is likely to have had some effect.

In a similar fashion, the state of Indiana's 20 percent copay on all spending between $2,750 and $8,000 very likely caused its participants to be more cautious with their spending than the people randomized into the RAND study's 95 percent copay group, because that group had a 0 percent copay after their deductible was reached.

Another reason to believe that randomization did not reduce the amount of cost savings has to do with the very obvious point that the RAND study lacked any health-savings component. Whereas the state of Indiana had HSAs *in addition to* high-deductible health insurance, the RAND study used only high-deductible health insurance. Thus, participants in the RAND study had only one reason to reduce spending: high out-of-pocket costs. By contrast, the people enrolled in the state of Indiana plan had two reasons to reduce spending: high out-of-pocket costs *and* the desire to preserve their health savings for a rainy day.

For those reasons, I am confident that the larger spending reduction achieved by Indiana was the result of the additional incentives provided by health savings plans, copays, and making people pay for 100 percent of all spending before their deductible was reached.

Chapter 23

Why Healthcare Spending Can Decline without Hurting Health Outcomes

In the previous chapters, you've seen how healthcare spending could be cut by 30 or even 36 percent without harming healthcare outcomes here in the United States. But even experts are stunned when they realize that Singapore has managed to provide the world's best healthcare while spending 50 to 60 percent less per person than the average developed country and 75 percent less than the United States. It doesn't seem possible that expenditures could be cut so dramatically without adversely affecting outcomes!

That perceived impossibility is based on the incorrect assumption that there is a strong relationship between healthcare spending and healthcare outcomes. The evidence, however, indicates that healthcare and medical services are only responsible for a small fraction of health outcomes, including the quality and duration of life. The large majority of health outcomes are actually the result of:

- Public health measures, such as clean drinking water and immunization programs;

- Economic factors, such as access to nutritious food and whether a person can get a job; and
- Social factors like the popularity of smoking, how likely people are to be literate, and whether people have supportive social networks.

To understand just how powerful these factors are in creating health and longevity, it is important to know that, of the thirty years by which life expectancy increased in the United States over the course of the twentieth century, twenty-five of those years were due to public health improvements such as immunizations, improved workplace safety, improved sanitation and hygiene, advances in food safety, the fluoridation of drinking water, increased transportation safety, and the drop in tobacco usage that began in the mid-1960s.[1]

To put things in proper perspective, consider New York City in 1900. Infectious diseases were rampant. The summer would bring epidemics of malaria and yellow fever, because the areas of New Jersey directly across the Hudson River were swamplands which bred billions of mosquitos. In response, the city's elite left each summer for cooler and healthier places like Bar Harbor, Maine, or Martha's Vineyard, Massachusetts. But the poor and middle class had to sit it out, hoping to avoid weeks spent in excruciating pain, possibly on the way to an early grave.

Sanitation was uniformly poor for all income levels. The city's 150,000 horses collectively dumped 3 million pounds of feces and 40,000 gallons of urine per day on the city's streets, creating a fly-swarmed mire of excrement, trash, and urine. There were giant rats, feral dogs, wild cats, and various carrion birds skulking about spreading diseases. Water was polluted. Food handling and refrigeration were haphazard at best. Most people lacked access to proper bathing and toilet facilities. And the poor were crowded into tiny apartments with poor heating, cooling, and ventilation.

The three leading causes of death were pneumonia, tuberculosis, and diarrhea—all communicable diseases, their spread facilitated by the era's cramped living conditions, wretched food safety, and inadequate sanitation. Out of a population of 3,665,825 people in 1900, 71,126 people died, resulting in an overall death rate of 1,940 per 100,000 people per year.[2] By comparison, New York City's 2010 population of 8,175,133 saw 52,575 deaths, for an overall death rate of 643 per 100,000 people.[3]

Looking at those numbers and the rest of New York City's historical mortality data, three things stand out:

- Even though New York City's population had more than doubled (from 3.7 million to 8.2 million), nearly 20,000 fewer people died in 2010 than in 1900 (52,575 vs. 71,126).
- New York City's death rate was more than three times higher in 1900 than in 2010 (1,940 per 100,000 vs. 643 per 100,000).
- The leading causes of death changed from communicable diseases affecting people of all ages to chronic diseasses associated with old age, such as heart disease and cancer.

The decline in mortality—and the reason why the vast majority of New Yorkers now live long enough to die of chronic diseases—was due to draining swamps and getting rid of mosquitoes; piping in clean drinking water to prevent cholera, dysentery and diarrhea; improving sewage and trash collection so people could safely dispose of waste; switching from horse-powered transportation to internal-combustion automobiles and electric subway cars; building ample housing with proper ventilation, heating, and sanitary facilities, so that even the poor could keep clean and warm; increasing literacy and education so that it became easy to spread information about public health, infant nutrition, and sanitation; and improving the farm-to-table food safety chain with reliable refrigeration, food inspection laws, and education about proper food-handling techniques, including washing one's hands before handling food.

Along with immunizations, these advances in public health acted to *prevent* disease. By contrast, healthcare and medicine come into play only *after* somebody gets sick. During the twentieth century, only a single medical or healthcare advance—antibiotics—made any major difference in health outcomes. Granted, antibiotics have saved millions of lives, and continue to do so today. But it was the preventive measures of public health rather than the curative measures of antibiotics that did the heavy lifting with respect to the twentieth century's historically unprecedented reductions in mortality and morbidity rates. Without the many advances in public health, we would be dying much sooner and much more painfully than we do today.

So when a person asks how Singapore can spend so much less on healthcare and medicine while still ending up with the world's best health outcomes, we need to point out that almost everybody incorrectly assumes that healthcare and medicine are the major drivers of health outcomes.

That false assumption is understandable, given how dramatically healthcare and medicine can help people who are already sick. As just one example, a single antibiotic injection can often save a seriously ill person from death. That is miraculous and unforgettable, especially if you are the one who is saved (as I was a couple of years ago after an infection caused by a bee sting spread rapidly up my leg). By contrast, almost nobody remembers the engineers who brought clean drinking water to New York City, the garbage collectors who today (and every day) cart away trash that would otherwise pile up and attract vermin, or the automobiles that we curse for global warming, without remembering how filthy horses were. The benefits of public health go unnoticed, their praises unsung.

Psychologists say that dramatic, easily remembered events have "high salience." Our healthcare debate has been hijacked by the high salience of modern medicine. But salience is not the same as effectiveness. We can cut back our expenditures on healthcare and medicine dramatically without adversely affecting health outcomes precisely because the major drivers of health outcomes are low-salience public health activities—activities too boring to remember.

Singapore takes the low-salience stuff seriously. Its Housing Development Board builds high-quality housing for the poor and middle classes. The water is clean; sanitation is excellent; pollution levels are low; people are encouraged to exercise; the food supply is safe; children are immunized; communicable diseases are under tight control. The government takes great pains to improve the economic and social factors that affect health and well-being. Jobs are plentiful. Smoking is discouraged. The government encourages supportive social networks by subsidizing community centers, non-profits, and recreational activities. The Ministry of Education also produces the world's best-educated young people, so spreading sophisticated scientific information about disease prevention is easy.

These efforts are low-salience but high-impact. They massively slash mortality and morbidity, but in a quiet way, and at a very low cost. Our healthcare and medical efforts are, by contrast, high-salience and low-impact. They only moderately reduce mortality and morbidity, but do so very flamboyantly and, in many cases, at a very high cost.

THE QUIET POWER OF PUBLIC HEALTH

The best way to understand how public health measures improve health outcomes cost-effectively is to realize that, over the course of the twentieth century, "clean water was responsible for nearly half the total mortality reduction in major cities, three-quarters of the infant mortality reduction, and nearly two-thirds of the child mortality reduction."[4] Clean water is cheap. The average price paid by Americans for tap water is two dollars per 1,000 gallons. Annual water and sewage charges average just $474 per household in the United States—or about fifty cents per person per day for the average-sized household.[5]

After clean drinking water, vaccinations have been the second most important cause of rising life expectancies and declining mortality rates.[6] Like clean water, vaccinations are cheap, with the cumulative cost of all recommended childhood immunizations from birth to age eighteen at just under $1,300 per child in the United States, or about $16.25 per year, if you assume that each child will reach eighty years of age. That $16.25 per year comes to just five cents per day over those eighty years.

Besides massively increasing life expectancy at extremely low costs, immunizations have also saved a lot of money in terms of weighing the dollar costs of prevention against the dollar costs of infection. Consider the measles. Just a single case of the measles costs $10,000 to treat, which includes the public health costs of investigation and containment. That's five hundred times more than the twenty dollars that it costs to inoculate a child with the MMR vaccine that protects not only against the measles but against mumps and rubella, too.

By contrast, the cost of medical interventions can easily run into the hundreds of thousands of dollars in the United States, even for common procedures like open-heart surgery and cancer treatment.

Their high costs looks even worse when you consider their benefits as measured in terms of increased life expectancy. Whereas public health measures have a huge impact on life expectancy because they prevent infant and child deaths, the large majority of costly medical and health interventions have only a modest effect on life expectancy because they go to middle-aged or elderly patients.

SPENDING ON THE VERY OLD

In particular, spending on the extremely elderly is typically a high-cost venture that does not deliver many added years of healthy life. In terms of raw numbers, 25 percent of annual Medicare expenditures go to elderly patients in the last year of life.[7] That's $145 billion per year—equivalent to 28 percent of all non-defense discretionary spending at the federal level. It's enough to cover the combined annual budgets of the Departments of Agriculture, Commerce, Energy, Interior, Labor, and Treasury plus the Army Corps of Engineers, the Environmental Protection Agency, NASA, the National Science Foundation, and the Social Security Administration.

Singapore has followed a different path by concentrating its healthcare efforts on the low-salience/high-impact stuff, rather than on the high-salience/low-impact stuff. At the national level, policymakers devote substantial resources to public health and prevention. At the individual level, first and second parties are presented with financial incentives that help avoid wasteful healthcare spending. Not least among these is the ability of Singapore's elderly to bequeath their unspent Medisave balances to their loved ones. That one policy difference means that older people in Singapore have a very different set of financial incentives when it comes to costly end-of-life treatments than older Americans who, from the age of sixty-five, have gotten used to Medicare picking up most of their healthcare costs.

PRUDENCE AND PREVENTION

Singapore's emphasis on prudent spending and good incentives also manifests in its cautious approach to preventive care, which employs routine checkups, counseling, and screening tests to try to catch health issues early, before they develop into serious conditions. In particular, Singapore's policy-makers are aware of a crucial problem: most types of preventive care do not reduce costs. Why? Because prevention is not free. You have to pay for a lot of screenings for a lot of people in order to be able to identify even one person to treat. The collective cost of those screenings in most cases equals or exceeds the future costs saved by providing early treatment to the subset of people whose conditions were detected by the screenings. You also run up a lot of unnecessary costs because people end up being falsely diagnosed when they are in fact perfectly healthy.

Besides all this, many commonly recommended preventive-care measures don't actually work. Consider general health exams and annual checkups. A meta-analysis of fourteen randomized studies published by the *British Medical Journal* in 2012 concluded that "general health checks did not reduce morbidity or mortality, neither overall nor for cardiovascular or cancer causes."[8] That alone is startling. What's worse, however, is that the same meta-analysis showed that patients randomized into receiving general checkups received up to 20 percent more diagnoses over the next six years—meaning they ran up more treatment costs, despite no improvements in either morbidity or mortality.

From a policy perspective, general checkups are a net loss for society. They increase medical spending without making the average person any healthier. And yet, many employer health insurance plans still incentivize participants to go in for regular, annual checkups. While I have no doubt about the good intentions of physicians who recommend annual checkups, the cynic in me wonders if the insurance companies themselves push wellness programs to increase spending and usage without actually delivering any improvements in either mortality or morbidity.

The cost-benefit situation of preventive care is so bad that one paper examining twenty "evidence-based" preventive services recommended by either the US Preventive Services Task Force or the Advisory Committee on Immunizations Practices found that if they were each applied to 90 percent of the US population, total US healthcare spending would fall by only 0.2 percent.[9]

Taken at face value, that 0.2 percent spending reduction is very discouraging. But if you dig a little deeper, the cost situation is even worse; four of the twenty preventive services had *no effect at all* on life expectancy, and only seven actually save any money. In fact, the vast majority of the benefits come from just one of the services (raising the childhood immunization rate to 90 percent). That one service provides about 79 percent of potential increases in life expectancy across all twenty interventions, as well as about 56 percent of the possible costs savings among the seven services that reduce costs. With childhood immunizations excluded, the other nineteen of these "proven" preventive services actually increase rather than lower US healthcare spending. And what's the potential gain for those extra costs? Just sixty-one days of additional life expectancy.[10]

These results demonstrate that preventive care is yet another aspect of healthcare in which higher spending does not translate into better outcomes or even lower net costs. To flip this around, we could, in many cases, lower net costs by doing *less* preventive care. That is certainly the case with general physical exams. Americans spend $8 billion on them every year. But as noted above, they improve neither morbidity nor mortality, while simultaneously generating more diagnoses that in turn lead to more treatments and higher medical spending.

Those extra treatments can have extremely negative personal consequences. Consider former Canadian Prime Minister Brian Mulroney. He was given a computer tomography (CT, or CAT) scan as part of a routine checkup in 2005. He felt perfectly fine, but the scan revealed two small lumps in his lungs. Fearing cancer, his doctors went in and removed the lumps. They turned out to be perfectly noncancerous, but the surgery caused Mulroney's pancreas to become so inflamed that he had to be put in intensive care. He spent six weeks in the hospital. Then, after being discharged, he had to come back a month later for another surgery to remove a pancreatic cyst that had been caused by the earlier inflammation. The net result? Many thousands of dollars in medical spending, nearly dying, and a long, painful recovery. All of it could have been avoided if Mulroney had known that those coming in for general health screenings don't do any better on average than those who don't.

Singapore's Ministry of Health has embraced this logic. It only encourages preventive screenings for conditions where there are clear net benefits, such as screenings for breast cancer and cervical cancer. Other screening exams are available, of course, but people must pay for them out of their own pockets. This provides a sensible financial incentive for both doctors and patients to run preventive screenings sparingly and only in cases that demonstrate a significant likelihood of doing more good than harm (as with patients who have a family history that biases them toward coming down with a particular condition).

Chapter 24

P, Q, and Big Savings for You

You've now seen how two variants of Singapore's healthcare system cut medical expenditures significantly right here in the United States. Costs fell 35 percent in the Indiana experiment and 30 percent in the RAND study. Of course, we'd prefer to save 35 percent, because more savings always sounds better. But even if we could only save 30 percent, we'd cut our healthcare spending from 17.9 percent of GDP down to only 12.5 percent of GDP. That would leave us with costs only moderately higher than France, the United Kingdom, and Canada (which spend between 9.4 and 11.7 percent of GDP on healthcare).

But, as I've told you, Singapore is spending just 4.2 percent of its GDP on healthcare—or about 75 percent less than we presently are. So let's consider the following question: *Why are we only finding 30 to 35 percent reductions on healthcare spending when Singapore is managing to make a 75 percent reduction from similar policies?*

The answer is very simple: You need to put *everybody* on Singapore-style health plans if you want to get the full 75 percent. If you only put a small part of the population on those plans, you only get a small part of the total possible cost reductions—30 to 35 percent rather than 75 percent.

To see why, let's dabble in a little accounting and algebra. (I promise it will be quick.)

The total expenditure (E) on any good or service is simply the quantity of the good consumed (Q) times the price per unit (P). Stated algebraically, $E = PQ$. For example, if you buy twenty-two apples at three dollars per apple, you will spend sixty-six dollars.

In the United States, our healthcare expenditures (E) are approaching $4 trillion per year. That total amount is the sum of a bunch of prices multiplied by a bunch of quantities (such as the price per rubber glove multiplied by the number of rubber gloves and the price per CT scan multiplied by the number of CT scans). Thus, our high total expenditure on healthcare can be conceptualized as high prices (P) times a lot of quantity consumed (Q).

Following that logic, the only way to reduce our total healthcare expenditure is to reduce either P or Q, or both; we must reduce the price per treatment, the number of treatments, or both.

The state of Indiana and RAND only managed 30 to 35 percent reductions in healthcare expenditures—rather than 75 percent reductions in healthcare expenditures—because they were limited by the small size of their participant groups. The small numbers of participants implied that Indiana and RAND only benefited from reductions in Q (rather than from reductions in P as well as Q). They weren't able to get any reductions in P because they didn't reduce the overall market demand for any particular good or service by an appreciable amount. Those large reductions in demand are only possible when a large fraction of consumers change their behavior.

For example, imagine that Walmart did something that you didn't like. Would the company even notice if you, by yourself, bought 30 to 35 percent less merchandise as a form of protest? Of course not. Walmart's revenues are north of $1 billion per day, so if one person cuts back 30 to 35 percent on how much he buys from Walmart, it wouldn't be noticeable.

Now imagine what would happen if you mounted a successful social media campaign that encouraged *everybody* in the country to purchase 30 to 35 percent fewer items at Walmart. Would Walmart notice that? Yes, of course it would. The demand for its products would crash, and in response, Walmart would have to put things on sale to lure people back. Prices would have to fall. Thus, there is a huge difference between one person (or a handful of people) cutting back on purchases and a large majority (or everybody) cutting back on purchases. Getting a substantial fraction of consumers to cut back on purchases is the only way to obtain a large decline in prices.

Consider how those economic realities play out with respect to the state of Indiana's CDHP plan. The state of Indiana has only thirty thousand employees. They constitute only about 1 percent of the state's entire labor force. So when 70 percent of Indiana's state employees joined the CDHP in its second year and cut their spending by 35 percent, healthcare providers didn't notice any change in overall market demand, because the resulting decrease in healthcare consumption amounted to less than one-third of one percent of total healthcare spending in the state of Indiana. As a result, medical prices stayed high for everybody.

Stated mathematically, P stayed the same in our equation $E = PQ$. The only reason that E fell was because Q fell. The 35 percent reduction in expenditures was due entirely to reductions in Q, the quantity of healthcare that was purchased.

But now think about what would happen if we enrolled *every* person in the state of Indiana into a Singapore-style CDHP plan. In that case, every consumer in Indiana would be reducing Q by 35 percent. That would represent such a massive decrease in the demand for healthcare services that P would *have* to fall.

Recall that emergency room and physicians visits fell 67 percent under the state of Indiana's CDHP. Imagine the shock to the system if *every* person in the state of Indiana went on that plan and also cut back by 67 percent. Such a colossal drop in usage would force hospitals to lower prices in an attempt to gain back some business.

If you put enough people on a Singapore-style plan, their combined decreases in usage will be enough to significantly lower prices. You will get declines not just in Q but in P as well. Both will decrease at the same time, with the result being massive declines in expenditures.

To see just how massive, you must keep in mind that P and Q are multiplied together in the expenditure equation $E = PQ$. When P and Q decline at the same time, they have synergistic, multiplicative effects on how quickly E falls. To see what I mean, suppose, for simplicity's sake, that medical procedures currently cost $100 each and that people are consuming 100 procedures in total. Expenditures would consequently be $10,000 ($100 per procedure times 100 procedures).

To show you how big the synergistic effects are from simultaneous declines in P and Q, let's first consider a case where there are no synergistic effects because there is a change in only one variable. Suppose that P remains at $100 per procedure but Q falls 35 percent, down to 65 procedures. Expenditures would consequently decline from $10,000 to only $6,500 ($100 per procedure times 65 procedures). This is what happened in Indiana. Its government workforce was too small to effect price declines, so the only factor reducing medical expenditures was the reduction in the quantity of healthcare services that they utilized.

But now imagine what would happen if we put every worker in the state on a Singapore-style plan and prices fell 20 percent, down to $80 per treatment. In that case, total expenditures on healthcare would fall to just $5,200 ($80 per treatment times 65 treatments). That's a big deal, as $5,200 is only about half of $10,000. To be exact, we've managed to achieve a 48 percent reduction in health-care expenditures, even though P and Q only fell individually by smaller percentages—35 percent in the case of Q, 20 percent in the case of P.

That much larger synergistic effect occurred because the reduction in each variable affected E directly, but also indirectly, by cutting down on the other variable's effect on E. That synergy means we don't have to cut healthcare prices by 75 percent to reduce health expenditures by 75 percent. We can cut prices by much less because we can be certain of getting 30 to 35 percent reductions in Q simply by switching people into Singapore-style healthcare plans.

Now, suppose P falls by 62.53 percent, down to $38.47 per treatment. Then the total expenditure on healthcare would be $2,500.55 ($38.47 per treatment times 65 treatments). That is almost exactly 75 percent less than the original $10,000 that was being expended in our example before we switched over to the Singapore-style CDHP. Thus, we know that we would need a decline in healthcare prices of about 62 percent to achieve Singapore-style reductions in healthcare spending.

The question then becomes: Are we likely to obtain 62 percent price declines in practice? I am confident that the answer is *yes*. First of all, it's been estimated that 31 percent of all healthcare spending in the United States is due to administrative costs—pushing insurance forms around and so on.[1]

By comparison, only 16.7 percent of healthcare spending in Canada goes to administrative costs. But a Singapore-style system should be able to beat that number easily, as Canada has a centralized, single-payer system, in which lots of paper has to be pushed around for every treatment because nothing in that system is cash and carry. By contrast, a large fraction of Singapore's healthcare spending is cash and carry, with no need for pushing paper around to bill third parties. So right off the bat, we should be able to save at least 20 percent just by reducing administrative costs.

Where to get the other 42 percent? Well, I don't think it will be that hard. To begin with, the price that you'd have to pay to get one of the Hoveround mobility scooters I discussed in an earlier chapter will fall precipitously when people have to pay for them from their own pockets, rather than having all or most of the cost picked up by a third party. The same is true for medical equipment, which is currently paid for either mostly or entirely by third parties.

Next, remember how in the state of Indiana the average cost per prescription fell $18 because so many more people opted for generic drugs rather than brand-name drugs? Well, imagine if we scaled that up to the whole economy. According to the Kaiser Family Foundation, there were 4,063,166,658 prescriptions filled at retail pharmacies in the United States in 2017.[2] (The total number of prescriptions filled throughout the United States was even higher, because a lot of prescriptions are filled via mail order these days. But to be conservative, let's base our estimates on the 4,063,166,658 retail prescriptions.)

If we had an $18-per-prescription decline for each of those prescriptions, we would see a $73 billion decrease in the amount of money spent on prescription drugs. That alone would decrease total healthcare spending by an additional 2.1 percent. (The actual amount of savings will be even higher, due to all those mail-order prescriptions that we ignored when making our estimate.) But no need to stop there. Once people are paying out of their own pockets for prescriptions, demand will decrease and prices will fall. The total amount saved on medicines would likely be several times larger than 2.1 percent.

Next, consider non-emergency, urgent-care types of situations— ear aches, sprained ankles, minor burns, cold symptoms, minor asthma attacks, etc. *Consumer Reports* puts the cost of taking care of those problems at an ER at about $400 a pop (including what the insurance company pays).[3] By contrast, urgent care centers usually charge about $120 for those sorts of services, while convenient care clinics (run inside of drug stores, supermarkets, and big-box retailers like Walmart) only charge between $55 and $75. If we put everybody on a Singapore-style, high-deductible plan where they had to spend their own money until they met the deductible, my guess is that we would see a massive change in behavior. People would head to urgent care centers and convenient care clinics rather than to the ER. That would not only save a ton of money, but it would also free up ER personnel to concentrate on actual emergencies.

How much money would reducing ER visits actually save, though? Well, let's consider some specific medical conditions and their costs at emergency rooms versus urgent care centers. To make the comparisons, we'll use 2013 data compiled by CareFirst BlueCross BlueShield, the giant insurance company that operates in the mid-Atlantic states.[4]

REDUCING ER VISITS AND COSTS

The average cost of treating acute bronchitis in an ER? $814. The average cost at an urgent care center? $122. That's *85 percent less.*

What about acute pharyngitis, that is, having a really sore throat? Well, that runs $620 at an ER, but only $93 at an urgent care center. Again, that's *85 percent less.*

What about low back pain? Also 85 percent less, costing $715 in the ER versus only $113 at an urgent care center.

Finally, let's look at something that plagued me as a kid: otitis media, or middle ear infections. Treatment runs $498 at ERs but only $100 at urgent care centers. (My parents would have appreciated that 80 percent cost savings back in the 1970s, when they had to haul me to the ER several times a year for ear infections; but urgent care centers did not yet exist.)

I should also say that wait times are far shorter at urgent care centers and convenient care clinics. Their patients typically wait less than twenty minutes to be seen, and they are treated and on their way only twenty minutes after that.[5] By comparison, people visiting ERs spend an average of two hours and fifteen minutes waiting to be seen and then actually being treated.[6] Most people also live much closer to the nearest urgent care center than to the nearest ER, so they also save on travel time.

The examples I've just given you only deal with the savings likely to arise from reducing administrative costs, spending less on pharmaceuticals, and utilizing less expensive primary-care providers. But what about the *really* expensive stuff—cancer treatments, open-heart surgeries, and so on? How much could we potentially save there? Well, if the prices in countries with medical tourism are any indication, the answer is: *boatloads*.

A heart bypass surgery will run about $130,000 in the United States. In Thailand? $11,000. Malaysia? $9,000. Singapore? $18,000.[7] And just to be clear, the quality is superb. You will be treated in state-of-the-art hospitals by American-trained surgeons, who are board-certified in the United States.

To be conservative, though, let's only compare the $130,000 cost for a heart bypass in the United States with the $18,000 cost in Singapore. Singapore is the only one of those three foreign countries to be fully industrialized and have the same sort of technologically advanced, high-wage economy as the United States. Indeed, the cost of living in Singapore is about 20 percent higher than in the United States. But despite those high labor costs, you can still get a heart bypass surgery done for 76 percent less in Singapore.

What about a hip replacement? That'll run you $43,000 in the good ol' US of A, but only $12,000 in Thailand, $10,000 in Malaysia, and $12,000 in Singapore. *It's 62 percent cheaper in Singapore!*

Need a knee replacement? It'll run you $40,000 in the United States, but only $10,000 in Thailand, $8,000 in Malaysia, and $13,000 in Singapore. Singapore's cost advantage? *67 percent!*

Heck, let's do one more: heart valve replacement. It will cost you $160,000 in the United States, but it will set you back only $10,000 in Thailand, $9,000 in Malaysia, and $12,500 in Singapore. The Singaporean cost-advantage to keep your blood pumping? *92.1 percent!*

All these medical-tourism numbers—especially those for high-labor-cost Singapore—show that if US medicine were made competitive by empowering first parties with spending power, we, too, would see the cost of major surgeries fall precipitously.

And that is another reason why I don't think we would have any trouble achieving a 62 percent decline in overall healthcare prices. If major surgeries cost between 62 and 92 percent less in Singapore, and primary care services costs 80 to 85 percent less at urgent care centers than at ERs, I don't see any reason why competitive pressures here in the United States should have any trouble reducing overall healthcare prices by 62 percent. We just need to get rid of our dependence on third-party payments and implement what works: well-funded health savings accounts coupled with high-deductible health insurance plans.

After people see how far prices are likely to fall under a Singapore-style healthcare system, I am often asked what doctors are paid in Singapore. The people asking me that question are afraid that, if Singapore is spending 75 percent less on healthcare overall, it mustn't have enough money to pay its doctors well.

As it turns out, however, Singapore's doctors are paid very well, with the median earnings of a general practitioner coming in at $154,400 per year, and specialists clocking in at $285,012 per year.[8] While those median earning figures are both about 30 percent less than the comparable US figures, Singaporean doctors make most of it back because Singapore's highest income tax rate is just 20 percent. And there are no state income taxes in Singapore, so the highest possible income tax rate is 20 percent. By contrast, most American states have income taxes that must be paid in addition to the federal income tax rate of 37 percent that applies to high earners.[9] So, on an after-tax basis, the salaries of Singapore's doctors are basically on par with the salaries of their US colleagues. Singapore's lower income tax rate makes up for Singapore's lower pre-tax salaries.

But this implies that someone else must be taking most of the financial hit from Singapore's massively lower healthcare expenditures. So who's taking it? It appears to be insurance companies, pharmaceutical companies, medical device makers, and other companies not directly providing medical services. With less paper to push, insurance companies need fewer employees. With so few people opting for brand-name drugs, Big Pharma has lower revenues. And with patients required to pay significant out-of-pocket costs for Hoverounds and other elective medical equipment, manufacturers sell fewer units at substantially lower prices. We've seen how rapacious these companies can be here in the United States. If these companies are the ones who have to take the "hit," what a boon for society!

Please note that Singapore's healthcare system cuts spending in a targeted way. Overhead costs and low-value items get weeded out while beneficial services remain. That's exactly what you'd expect from a system that asks first parties to spend their own money and to consider whether benefits exceed costs.

One final point: Singapore's healthcare system has implemented a wide variety of strategies for keeping costs and prices down. When it comes to emulating Singapore's methods as a way to reduce our own costs, there is no shortage of practices to imitate. For example, besides health-savings accounts, high-deductible health insurance, and robust competition, we could also copy Singapore's decision to put public-sector doctors on fixed annual salaries, thereby removing from them the financial incentive to increase their incomes by ordering more tests or recommending more procedures. We could make each public hospital its own independent non-profit, so that public healthcare institutions would be forced to compete for clients but still have independent budgetary and management rights that allow them to compete and thrive. There's also a large opportunity presented by Singapore's willingness to separate quality care from cushy accommodations; we too could get the rich to voluntarily pay more, and then use that money to subsidize the healthcare of the poor.

So when it comes to cutting back health expenditures, we do not have to rely solely on *P* and *Q* falling. There are many other ways in which competition, choice, and sensible payment policies could help to massively reduce the amount of money we currently spend on healthcare. Those reforms will also raise quality, reduce waiting times, and improve customer service.

Chapter 25

You Have to
Fund People's HSAs
for Them

Because human brains are overly focused on short-term gains rather than long-term benefits, policy-makers must in one way or another compel people to save for future healthcare expenses, because people won't get around to saving enough if they are left to their own devices. To that end, Singapore openly and explicitly requires people to put money into their MediSave Accounts. But the necessary savings can also be obtained covertly, by having employers deposit money into employees' health savings accounts, as is done by Whole Foods Market, the state of Indiana, and 71 percent of all firms offering consumer-directed healthcare plans (CDHPs).

Workers don't think of those deposits as compulsory savings, because it looks like the money they are getting is an additional fringe benefit or perk that they receive from their employer. But in a competitive labor market, any money that a firm puts into a health savings account would have otherwise flowed to workers, either as higher take-home pay or as increased employer spending on other types of fringe benefits, such as day care or life insurance. So what is really going on when firms deposit money into workers' health savings accounts? The workers are being forced to save for future health expenses rather than being allowed to freely spend the money as they would have had it been given to them as wages, salaries, or other types of fringe benefits.

The trouble with letting workers do whatever they please with their total compensation package is that human beings suffer from what behavioral economists refer to as "decision-making myopia," or the tendency to focus on short-term options to the detriment of longer-term opportunities. As an example, consider college savings. Even if Joe knows that he should be saving $500 per month for his kids' college fund, he will constantly be tempted to spend that money on things that will bring immediate enjoyment or benefit to either him or his family—nicer Christmas presents for the kids, a romantic hot-air balloon ride for his wife, new tires for the convertible, etc.

Now, you might hope that Joe's wife will be a better planner and saver than he is, but, unfortunately, nearly everyone is myopic in their decision making. We all tend to favor now over later. As a result, we also tend to both under-save and overspend.

The tendency to under-save is lethal for purely voluntary CDHPs. You can offer a high-deductible health insurance plan in combination with a health savings account, but most people will not save nearly enough on their own to be able to cover the annual deductible and copays. If they are later hit with those expenses, they will find themselves having to beg or borrow money—or sell or hock assets—to make up the shortfall.

Alternatively, they may just forgo treatment, as has been a problem with many Affordable Care Act participants who have found themselves without the money necessary to pay their deductibles and copays.[1] Indeed, a 2014 study by the Commonwealth Fund found that about 60 percent of privately insured adults with low incomes reported that "it was difficult or impossible to afford their deductible."[2] Even worse, "46 percent of insured adults with incomes under 200 percent of poverty said that, because of their copayments or coinsurance, they had either not filled a prescription, not gone to the doctor when they were sick, skipped a medical test or follow-up visit recommended by a doctor, or not seen a specialist when they or their doctor thought they needed one."

Putting people into CDHPs without ensuring that they are going to have enough money to pay for their deductibles and copays creates a medically underserved group that will be highly displeased with their health insurance. They *could* blame their own myopia for not having saved enough—but that's probably not how they will react, especially if they are poor and have not had much of a chance to save up any money on their own. Instead, they will probably feel that the system is hideously costly, unfair, and inefficient. They will demand traditional insurance with negligible out-of-pocket costs; they will want to lock in our hideously expensive third-party payments system; and they may even find themselves favoring Canadian and UK-style single-payer options, such as "Medicare for All."

Ironically, their decision-making myopia reinforces their demand for traditional insurance. Because of myopia, they will be eager to select a short-run option (*Hurray! No out-of-pocket spending!*) because their myopic minds will discount the superior long-run option (*We're only spending 4.2 percent of GDP on healthcare! And my taxes are lower! And I am healthier! And everybody I love is going to live longer! Hurray!*)

Singapore compensates for that myopia by requiring everyone to save. Money flows automatically into people's MediSave Accounts. Those savings form a nest egg that sufficiently covers MediShield's premiums, deductibles, and copays for the vast majority of savers. As a result, participants don't end up short of money or massively resentful about being on a high-deductible health insurance plan.

Singapore's experience teaches us that if you want to make a CDHP system both workable and palatable, the quantity of automatic savings has to be large enough to cover the system's premiums, deductibles, and copays, except in the most unfortunate situations of catastrophic healthcare spending or deep poverty (in which case an institution like MediFund should take over). Whether you want the automatic savings to be overt, as with MediSave, or covert, as with employer HSA contributions, is not of primary importance. What matters is making sure that the total amount saved is large enough to overcome people's inability to save enough on their own. Once that is achieved, there will only ever be a modest amount of political agitation for lower deductibles, lower copays, or single-payer systems offering first-dollar coverage for each and every possible medical treatment.

Chapter 26

We Must Rescue the Poor from Medicaid

Switching to a Singapore-style healthcare system would also improve the health of America's poor and needy by finally retiring Medicaid. As background, recall that people randomized into receiving Medicaid in the state of Oregon did no better on measured health outcomes than those who were not randomized into Medicaid. That might leave you thinking that even though the Oregon Medicaid patients spent 36 percent more, they at least were not harmed by entering Medicaid. Unfortunately, however, many studies find that Medicaid actually hurts the poor by *increasing* mortality and morbidity.

To begin with, a study in the journal *Cancer* reported that Medicaid patients *and* people totally lacking any form of health insurance were both 50 percent more likely to die than patients who had private health insurance.[1] So being on Medicaid doesn't just increase your likelihood of dying, it's also no better than being totally without insurance.

That by itself would be pretty bad, but some other studies indicate that being on Medicaid is actually *worse* than being totally without insurance. A major University of Virginia study published in the *Annals of Surgery* found that individuals enrolled in Medicaid are almost twice as likely to die after surgery as privately insured patients, and about one-eighth more likely to die than the uninsured.[2] Yes, you read that correctly: *Medicaid patients are one-eighth more likely to die than the uninsured*. So Medicaid delivers both high costs *and* horrific outcomes.

Even worse, that wasn't the only study to show that Medicaid patients had worse outcomes than the uninsured. A study published in the *American Journal of Cardiology* found that Medicaid patients had major subsequent heart attacks after angioplasty twice as often as people who had no health insurance.[3]

Medicaid patients undergoing lung transplants also suffer. According to a study in the *Journal of Heart and Lung Transplantation*, Medicaid patients were 8.1 percent less likely to survive ten years after the surgery than either the privately insured or the uninsured.[4] So again, Medicaid patients do even worse than the uninsured.

Please note that in each of these studies, researchers controlled for demographic factors, initial health status, location, comorbidities, etc. So the results *cannot* be explained away by assuming that the people on Medicaid were sicker to begin with. Even after taking their initial health status into account, Medicaid patients did worse than the uninsured. Perhaps we shouldn't be surprised that 60 percent of Oregon's Medicaid lottery winners didn't bother to turn in their applications. Maybe they knew from talking to others that Medicaid can be a poison rather than a palliative.

But why does Medicaid end up hurting rather than helping? Probably because it refuses to pay nearly enough to get its recipients good service. To see just how little Medicaid pays, look at Figure 26.1, which is a map of the United States that shows the ratio for each state of how much Medicaid reimburses (pays) medical service providers for primary care relative to how much those primary care providers get on average from private insurance companies for identical services. The ratios differ by state because Medicaid is a joint state/federal program and each state has latitude in deciding who gets covered and how generous (or not!) that coverage will be.

Let's start with Texas, which is easy to spot on the map. It's 0.55 ratio means that its Medicaid system only pays 55 cents for every dollar that private insurance pays. That low ratio gives you some idea of the difficulties that Medicaid patients have when competing against people with private insurance for the limited supply of medical services. The low ratio also makes Texas look bad.

Figure 26.1: Medicaid Reimbursement Rates for Primary Care Relative to Private Insurance

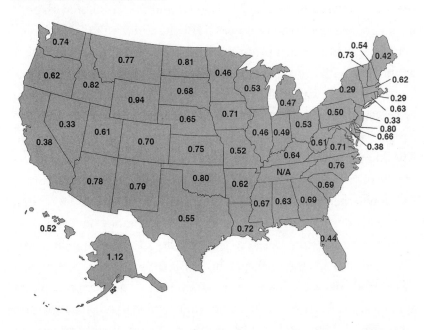

Source: "How Do Blue States Expand Medicaid? By Paying Doctors Less" by Avik Roy, Forbes.com, July 23, 2012.

As it turns out, however, many other states make Texas look rather generous. California's Medicaid system only pays 38 cents on the dollar versus private insurance, while New York's Medicaid system only pays 29 cents on the dollar versus private insurance.

If you're wondering whether there's any rhyme or reason to the huge variations in Medicare payout ratios, there is. The progressive politicians in "blue" states generally try to maximize the number of people who can qualify for Medicaid, but they normally don't have more money than the politicians in conservative "red" states. So the money has to be spread more thinly. The result is lower reimbursement rates in "blue" states.

Looking across all states, it is not surprising that nearly one-third of primary care doctors admit that they refuse to take new patients whose only health insurance is Medicaid.[5] Children are among the many victims. A survey of specialty clinics in Chicago published in the *New England Journal of Medicine* found that children with public health insurance (Medicaid or CHIP, the Children's Health Insurance Program) were six times as likely to be denied an appointment as children with private health insurance.[6]

The survey was conducted over the phone by researchers who pretended to be mothers of young children. These "secret shoppers" called doctors' offices to schedule appointments for their children. The point was to see what questions were asked by the people answering the phones at the doctors' offices. In particular, researchers wanted to see whether children in need of appointments would be treated differently depending on the type of health insurance they had.

The *first* question posed to the majority of secret shoppers was, "What kind of insurance do you have?" If the secret shoppers replied "Medicaid" or "CHIP," they usually were not allowed to schedule an appointment. And even when clinics were willing to schedule appointments for children with public health insurance, their average wait times were more than twice as long—forty-two days on average for the callers who replied that their children had public health insurance, versus twenty days for those who replied that their children had private health insurance.

Our Medicaid system is awful. The best way to help the poor would be to get rid of it and let all Americans—rich and poor—participate in a single system, just as Singapore uses MediShield as a single system for both the rich and poor. Having a separate system for the poor is far too susceptible to underfunding and neglect by politicians, who often only pay lip service to providing the needy with quality healthcare.

Singapore's system provides the best evidence that high-deductible health insurance combined with health savings is wonderfully effective in helping the poor. But just in case you have any doubts that such a system would work over here too, let me tell you about something else Mitch Daniels did when he was governor of Indiana.

You see, he implemented not only the Singapore-style, CDHP health insurance plan for government employees that we discussed at length in an earlier chapter, but also a separate Singapore-style, CDHP health insurance plan for the state's poor. It's called the Healthy Indiana Plan (HIP) and has been administered since 2007 under a waiver from the Department of Health and Human Services. The waiver allowed the state of Indiana to offer this innovative solution as part of Indiana's Medicaid program, even though it varies greatly from traditional Medicaid.

As with Singapore's 3Ms, the Healthy Indiana Plan has not received the media coverage it deserves. Of the attention it has received, my favorite piece on HIP was published in *Forbes* by Avik Roy, founder and president of the Foundation for Research on Equal Opportunity.[7] Let me quote Roy's key paragraphs:

Beneficiaries get a high-deductible health plan and a health savings account, called a POWER account, to which individuals must make a mandatory monthly contribution between 2 to 5 percent of income, up to $92 per month. Participants lose their coverage if they don't make their contributions within 60 days of their due date. After making this contribution, beneficiaries have no other cost-sharing requirements (co-pays, deductibles, etc.) except for non-urgent use of emergency rooms. The state chips in $1,100, which corresponds to the size of the would-be deductible.

Those who have money remaining in their POWER accounts at the end of the year can apply the balance to the following year's contribution requirements, if they have obtained a specified amount of preventive care: annual physical exams, pap smears and mammograms for women, cholesterol tests, flu shots, blood glucose screens, and tetanus-diphtheria screens.

"We did a lot of reading on criticism of health savings accounts," says Seema Verma, who was the architect of the Indiana program. "One of the criticisms was that people didn't have enough money to pay for preventive care. So we took preventive care out, made that first-dollar coverage. Also, people said that people didn't have enough for the deductible, so we fully funded it. Then, you have to make your contribution every month, with a 60-day grace period. If you don't make the contribution, you're out of the program for 12 months. It's a strong personal responsibility mechanism."

The program has been, by many measures, a smashing success. "What we're finding out is that, first of all, low-income people are just as capable as anybody else of making wise decisions when it's their own money that they're spending," Mitch Daniels explains in a Heritage Foundation video. "And they're also acting more like good consumers. They're visiting emergency rooms less, they're using more generic drugs, they're asking for second opinions. And some real money is starting to accumulate in their [health savings] accounts."

The program has been overwhelmingly popular in Indiana. There's a large waiting list—in the tens of thousands—to enroll in Healthy Indiana; enrollment was capped in order to ensure that the program's costs remain predictable. 90 percent of enrollees are making their required monthly contributions. "The program's level of satisfaction is at an unheard-of 98 percent approval rating," Verma told Kenneth Artz. Employers didn't dump their workers onto the program, crowding others out, because you needed to be uninsured for six months in order to be eligible for it.

A 2010 study by Mathematica Policy Research found that the program dramatically increased the percentage of beneficiaries who obtained preventive care, from 39 percent in the first six months of enrollment to 59 percent after one year. Of the members who had money left in the POWER accounts at the end of the year, 71 percent met the preventive care requirement and were able to roll the balances over to the following year. (The remaining 29 percent could roll over their personal contributions, but not the state contributions to their POWER accounts.)

This is an astounding achievement, given that the biggest problem with Medicaid is the way that it ghettoizes its participants, preventing them from gaining access to routine medical and dental care. This lack of physician access is the biggest reason why health outcomes for Medicaid patients lag far behind those of individuals with private insurance, and even behind those with no insurance at all. Healthy Indiana has completely reversed this trend, achieving preventive care participation rates that are *higher* than the privately-insured population.[8]

Thanks to the Healthy Indiana Plan, we know that Singapore-style health plans will work here in America just as well for the poor as for the rich. But again, I do not advocate for two separate Singapore-style systems, one for the rich and one for the poor. History warns us that "separate but equal" is a lie. If we are to build a universal system that delivers quality care to one and all, we cannot have two systems.

Chapter 27

Visiting the Free Market
Medical Association

Every year, there is a weekend conference in Oklahoma or Texas hosted by Dr. Keith Smith, the founder of the Surgery Center of Oklahoma. A visit to this conference is a great way to learn how a few thousand rebels in the American healthcare industry have managed to fight back against the high costs, low quality, and poor access generated by third-party payments. A visit to the conference is also a good reminder that the healthcare policies that work so well in Singapore were invented here in America and work just as well here in America.

In addition to running the Surgery Center of Oklahoma—a medical facility that posts all of its prices online—Dr. Smith is the president of the Free Market Medical Association, which counts among its members medical doctors, insurance brokers, and groups like Christian Healthcare Ministries that provide an innovative alternative to traditional health insurance.

Dr. Smith is an anesthesiologist by training, but he and the forty other physicians who are partners in the Surgery Center provide over 280 different surgical procedures—everything from C-sections to cataract surgeries to knee replacements to thyroidectomies. The Surgery Center of Oklahoma posts all-inclusive prices for each surgery as part of its goal to provide complete price transparency and account-ability. If a patient's case gets complicated and there are cost overruns, that is the Surgery Center's problem. The patient only has to pay the price posted online.

The Surgery Center's prices are low because it does as much insurance-free, cash-and-carry, first-party-payment business as pos-sible. It saves large amounts of money by not having to deal with the costs, delays, and staffing needs associated with third-party health insurance billing and claims processing. The Surgery Center can concentrate on providing medical services and figuring out how to deliver them at the lowest possible costs while maintaining world-class quality.

The Surgery Center's prices are so low that it has single-handedly created an inbound medical tourism industry in Tulsa, Oklahoma, where it is located. Patients fly in from places as far afield as Canada, Europe, Central America, and the Caribbean for surgical services.

Dr. Smith started posting all-inclusive prices online in 2009. In 2014, he founded the Free Market Medical Association with his friend Jay Kempton. Kempton runs a non-profit called Advantage Health Plans Trust that helps community banks provide healthcare coverage to their employees. From the employees' perspective, that coverage looks like high-deductible health insurance coupled with a health savings account. But there's a twist. No insurance companies are involved. Rather, Kempton helps community banks create self-funded health plans that they control and pay for themselves.

To do so, each community bank estimates its likely exposure to healthcare costs—how much it will have to pay for its employees' healthcare in excess of their respective annual deductibles. As an example, a bank in Enid, Oklahoma would hire an actuary to estimate probable healthcare scenarios for its pool of employees and thus how much its employees as a group are likely to spend on healthcare in a given year.

In some scenarios, they will be quite healthy and run up only modest healthcare expenses. In other scenarios, employees will get sick much more often, or come down with lots of costly conditions. It's the actuary's job to figure out which scenarios are the most likely to occur. The actuary will also calculate how big the Enid bank's financial exposure will be under each scenario.

Suppose that the "most likely" exposure amount turns out to be $2.2 million. To deal with that $2.2 million liability, the Enid bank should set aside $2.2 million. But there is always the possibility that workers will get sicker than average and run up higher costs than average. To deal with the possibility of higher costs, Mr. Kempton will recommend that the bank purchase a "stop-loss" insurance plan that will pay for any expenses above $2.2 million. By doing so, the bank can be sure that it won't be blindsided if its employees collectively have an abnormally expensive year when it comes to healthcare costs.

The community banks that work with Kempton also typically create health savings accounts for their employees and then donate generously into those accounts. The result is a system that shares the same good incentives as the Whole Foods Market healthcare plan, the Healthy Indiana Plan, and Singapore's 3Ms. Participants are provided with deductible security while also being presented with a reason to shop around and spend prudently (since any unspent HSA balances are theirs to keep and roll over to the next year).

If you go to a Free Market Medical Association meeting, you will find at least a half dozen firms like Kempton's that can advise companies on how to set up their own self-funded health plans using stop-loss insurance. They can also provide debit card services to manage HSA funds and do the paper pushing necessary to deal with claims in excess of the annual deductible. The result is a quick and easy way for any firm to have an expense-slashing alternative to traditional health insurance.

Christian Healthcare Ministries and several similar companies offer a different alternative to traditional insurance, one designed for individuals and families directly (rather than for companies wishing to offer self-funded health plans to their employees). Christian Healthcare Ministries (CHM) was founded in 1981 as a non-profit, voluntary, cost-sharing organization in which participants cover each other's medical bills. A crucial point must be made here: CHM is not an insurance company. It is a system in which participants make voluntary donations into a common pool that will be used to pay for future healthcare expenses. If a participant subsequently has a medical incident, they can apply to the pool for reimbursement for any amount above a per-incident deductible. The result is a system that functions like high deductible health insurance coupled with health savings accounts.

There is a major difference, though, between what CHM does and what traditional health insurance companies do. Traditional health insurance companies are legally obligated to pay out on any claim that meets the terms set out in the insurance agreement. But CHM can use its own discretion in evaluating reimbursement requests—even to the point, in theory, of denying a request without explanation. That crucial difference frees CHM from being regulated as an insurance company, and thus allows it to avoid costly insurance regulations and overhead. Costs are also kept under control by asking participants to shop around whenever possible before obtaining medical services services and to pay for costs themselves before asking for reimbursements.

The fact that participants must front their own money before requesting a reimbursement means that they are very careful comparison shoppers. And they are not alone in their comparison shopping. CHM has full-time employees whose only job is to help participants call around to local providers to negotiate the lowest possible prices *in advance* for everything from blood work to major surgeries. The result is a system that strongly favors prudence and low-cost providers.

Millions of people have participated in CHM, which has paid out more than $2.5 billion worth of reimbursement requests. If you go to a Free Market Medical Association meeting, a CHM representative will explain the details of CHM participation and how participants can select from a variety of plans with different deductible levels. Those plans are all much less expensive than traditional health insurance, because the bad incentives for overspending associated with third-party insurance payments are strongly controlled by CHM's requirement that costs be fronted by participants before a reimbursement request can be filed.

A Free Market Medical Association meeting also has several educational sessions explaining how physicians can break free of our traditional health insurance system. One option is Direct Primary Care (DPC), in which a primary care doctor charges her patients a fixed monthly retainer that covers annual checkups and routine office visits (such as for sore throats and sprained ankles) while tacking on additional charges as needed for things like blood tests, X-rays, and house calls. Monthly retainers typically run $100 to $200 per month per family, and DPC physicians have typically identified the lowest cost providers for outside services.

A key benefit to the DPC system is that DPC physicians can typically spend more time with each patient during an office visit than non-DPC physicians can. The monthly retainer means that DPC doctors are not under massive pressure to see as many patients as possible, as quickly as possible, in order to run as many billing codes as possible, in order to cover costs and make a living. DPC physicians can spend as much time with each patient as is medically optimal. They are also freed from the costs and staffing needs associated with processing insurance claims.

Many DPC clients have traditional health insurance coverage, but they are willing to pay a monthly DPC retainer in order to get reliable, twenty-four-hour, on-call access to a trusted physician. No need to wait weeks to get an appointment. No need to go to urgent care or an emergency room because they can't get a doctor on the phone. With DPC, patients have quick and reliable access to all types of primary healthcare services.

The Free Market Medical Association's seminars on DPCs are directed at physicians and largely concern running a small business. This business training is necessary because most of today's medical doctors have never been independent businesspeople. They have spent their careers as salaried employees in a system dominated by third-party payments. It takes training for them to learn how to deal with first-party payments and cater to the needs of first-party patients rather than third-party insurance companies.

DPC doctors have to attract and retain enough paying clients to make a living. That takes marketing and sales efforts in addition to providing popular services at an attractive price. By contrast, the vast majority of American physicians are paid, either directly or indirectly, by insurance companies whose "approved provider networks" channel patients to doctors automatically.[1]

Direct Primary Care is, in many ways, a return to what medical care looked like before the American healthcare system came to be dominated by third-party payments and insurance billing codes. Only a few decades ago, the large majority of doctors were businesspeople running private practices or small group practices. They knew their patients personally, could spend as much time with each one as was necessary, and could even customize their fees based on each patient's ability to pay—charging more to richer patients while charging much less or nothing to poorer patients. That regime was slowly killed off by the overweening bureaucracy required to run a huge system dependent on third-party payments. Private practices disappeared as the overhead costs of processing insurance claims grew and grew and grew again.

Doctors also had to shorten the time spent with each patient in order to see as many patients as possible to run as many billing codes as possible in order to make a living. And that got harder each year because Medicare, Medicaid, and private insurers habitually and continually cut the reimbursement rates for individual procedures. The only way for doctors to make up for being reimbursed a smaller amount per procedure is to run more procedures and billing codes through the system. Direct Primary Care returns personalized care and expertise to the patient-physician relationship by eschewing third-party payments and billing codes as much as possible.

Americans should be comfortable with all the reforms suggested in this book, because they were almost all invented here in America. Consider health savings accounts. Their inventor, economist John Goodman, is still very much alive and pushing hard for market-based healthcare reforms. High-deductible health insurance was also invented in America. So was the price tag, which is crucial for comparison shopping and promoting competition among providers.[2] The Free Market Medical Association has led the charge for first-party payments, posted prices, and high-deductible health insurance coupled with health savings accounts. This book will hopefully help them spread the word about how much better healthcare could be—and how much less it would cost—if we simply embraced these great methods that we invented here in the United States.

Chapter 28

My Proposal for Reforming the US Healthcare System

A great variety of healthcare reform plans have been suggested for America over the past seventy years. Some, like Medicare, Medicaid, and the Affordable Care Act, were even implemented. Today, suggestions range all the way from UK-style single-payer national health systems ("Medicare for All") to German-style compulsory insurance systems.

My reform proposal rests on the proven combination of high-deductible health insurance and health-savings accounts. As you now know, the health-savings accounts cover routine expenses, premiums, deductibles, and copays, while the high-deductible health insurance shields people from medical-spending catastrophes. Placing spending decisions in the hands of individual consumers encourages competition, drives down prices, and increases efficiency. Those benefits allow Singapore to deliver the world's best healthcare while spending 75 percent less than what America spends.

My plan is designed to obtain those same benefits and ensure that the system we create meets our deep-seated desire to provide universal coverage, equal access, and a real safety net. My plan will deliver high quality, affordability, and peace of mind, as well as equity, fairness, and universal coverage.

There are three key elements. The first is price transparency, so that competition can flourish. The second is the pairing of high-deductible health insurance with fully funded health savings accounts. The third is the use of age-rated—rather than community-rated—health insurance.

PRICE TAGS AND THE POWER OF "PUSHING" PRICE INFORMATION

You have already seen the benefits of price tags and price transparency in terms of lowering costs and raising quality. LASIK is the most famous example, but every medical procedure that is "elective," and thus not covered by health insurance, follows the same pattern: providers looking to increase sales must work hard to find ways to increase quality and lower prices. They must compete. And when they do, we reap the natural benefits of authentic competition: increased supply, reduced prices, and improved quality.

Please note that those three benefits are the result of the competitive pressures confronting providers. One common complaint about price tags and price transparency is that providing consumers with price information doesn't seem to have much of an effect on what they buy or from whom they buy. The vast majority of consumers either don't use the data or don't seem to be affected by the data.[1]

The researchers who point this out—and it is true as far as it goes—then draw the wrong conclusion. They assume that posting prices will have no beneficial effects. But we have seen again and again with elective procedures that prices do fall and quality does rise when prices are available. That seems to imply a contradiction, but only if you fail to miss the additional fact that the benefits of price transparency result from actions taken by providers, not consumers.

When prices are posted publicly, providers worry that they will lose business if they don't find a way to undercut their competition with lower prices. So, they work hard to slash costs and reduce prices. And once those cuts are made, competitors must respond by figuring out a way to match those innovations, lest they get priced out of the market.

But, again, you might wonder how a competitor could get "priced out of the market" if the majority of consumers seem indifferent to looking up pricing data and using it to comparison shop. The key to resolving the paradox is to understand that the systems which provide consumers with price-comparison information are "pull systems" rather than "push systems." A pull system, with respect to price transparency, is one in which I, the consumer, have to go out and find the relevant prices myself. A non-profit or my insurance company may have posted the information for me online, but I still have to take the time to find it, read it, and use it. That is unlikely to happen, given how busy people are and how much information overload we are already having to deal with.

By contrast, a push system delivers pricing information *to* me, without my having to do anything. Advertising is a push system. Providers of LASIK and other elective procedures push their prices to consumers via paid advertising. The information comes to the consumer, rather than the consumer having to go to the information.

Even better, the providers have a personal financial incentive to get this information to consumers. Providers know they can increase their sales and profits by advertising high quality at low prices to their consumers. And we can expect more of that proactive behavior if we insist on price tags for everything in healthcare.[2]

To that end, I propose legislation mandating that every provider of medical services be required to post prices. In addition, posted prices would apply to all consumers equally. The current practice of charging different prices to different patients for exactly the same service or procedure must end. Everyone will get charged the same price for the same service or procedure. Competition will flourish in that environment, as high-priced providers will need to worry about low-cost rivals pushing pricing information out into the marketplace in order to steal market share.

One final point on posted prices: the services sold at those posted prices should generate most of a provider's income. Under our current insurance billing system, providers get paid mostly by third parties, so providers have no incentive to advertise prices to first parties. That will change when the spending decisions made by first parties become determinative. When that becomes the norm, providers will have to compete for first-party spending. They will push pricing information out to consumers while also figuring out how to deliver higher quality at lower prices. This is what happens now with elective procedures like LASIK, and it is what will happen system-wide if we insist on posted prices and first-party payments.

PRICE TAGS SLASH COSTS BY ELIMINATING BARTERING AND HAGGLING

The use of price tags doesn't just encourage competition; it has the additional benefit of massively reducing costs by eliminating the need for bartering and haggling. To understand why bartering and haggling are so costly, consider the sort of old-fashioned open-air markets or bazaars that still exist in many countries. Often, an American tourist will attempt to purchase a local handicraft, such as a blanket, at such a market. But there are no price tags. All of the prices must be negotiated.

If you are serious about the process and want to try to get a good price, you will have to invest at least ten to twenty minutes haggling, bartering, and negotiating over the price. That includes theatrical tactics, like walking away to feign indifference and starting the negotiation by offering a comically low amount that no seller would ever accept. The seller will counter with a ridiculously high price that you would never accept. Ten to twenty minutes after first perusing the wares, you will have finally negotiated a price.

You may think to yourself: "Whew! Thank goodness that's over!"

But what if you wanted to comparison shop? What if you wanted prices from each of the other people selling blankets at the open-air market? Well, in that case, you would have to spend ten to twenty minutes haggling with each seller, in sequence, in order to get a price from each seller so that you could comparison shop.

That process of serial haggling is incredibly costly in both time and labor—and is best avoided, if possible.

Fortunately for the modern world, an American entrepreneur named John Wanamaker invented the price tag during the 1860s, thereby eliminating the time and labor costs associated with bartering and haggling. He would also go on to invent the money-back guarantee, build the first department store in Philadelphia, and run the first copyrighted advertisement, which allowed him to introduce another novel concept to the public: truth in advertising.

Our medical system is, by contrast, a barter system *without* truth in advertising. When you see a hospital billing a patient twenty-five dollars for a Tylenol, that is not "truth in advertising." The Tylenol did not cost the hospital that much. The opacity of our current medical billing system allows all sorts of shenanigans to take place, all to the benefit of connected insiders, including pharmaceutical companies, device manufacturers, and even the people who wholesale Tylenol. Their ability to outrageously inflate the prices of even common items is based entirely on the fact that there are no price tags available for anything covered by health insurance. Give patients prices in advance, and nobody would be able to charge twenty-five dollars for a single tablet of Tylenol. Patients would refuse to pay that amount because they know they can get an entire bottle of Tylenol for under ten dollars at their local pharmacy.

The universal availability of price tags would also make comparison shopping easy, especially in our internet era, since prices can be posted online for easy comparison. Ideally, you would be able to type the name of any medical service into an app and instantly get price quotes from every local provider. You would then press a button to schedule an appointment at the provider you liked best. None of that is currently possible because our current healthcare financing system plays a constant game of "Hide the Prices."

Price tags would also slash the hidden costs of bartering and haggling, which constitute a massive portion of healthcare spending in the United States. To see just how big those costs are, consider the process by which a person with insurance, like myself, gets billed for medical services covered by insurance. As a concrete example, let me tell you about a visit to a local doctor that I made about five years ago.

I needed a minor surgery done and went to a local specialist. He performed major surgeries at San Antonio Hospital in Upland, California, but he also had his own little office across the street in an office park. His office had four employees: the doctor himself, plus three women. One was middle-aged, like the doctor. She answered the phone, scheduled patients, and performed all duties necessary to running the office, including making sure the rent got paid and the payroll got processed.

After my little procedure was done, I inquired with the doctor about the two other employees. They were in their twenties, and it wasn't clear to me what they did, since neither of them was assisting patients in any way. The doctor was the only one in the office providing healthcare services, so what did those two employees do?

The doctor explained that their only tasks were to process insurance forms and obtain insurance company pre-approvals for drug prescriptions. All they did was push paper, fill out electronic forms, and call insurance companies. They provided no care to patients.

After returning home from that office visit, it struck me that we had created a healthcare system in which a single provider of medical services had to be backed up by two full-time employees whose only job was to process third-party payments. That is, of course, very costly. The two employees had to be provided with two salaries, two sets of retirement benefits, and two sets of healthcare benefits to provide insurance-billing support for a single provider of medical services.

The next morning, I woke up and realized that things were actually even worse. If there were two people in the doctor's office shoving insurance forms out the door, there logically had to be two people on the other end receiving and processing those forms. America had created a healthcare system in which it took *four* people pushing insurance forms around to back up each person actually providing healthcare services!

That level of profligacy is the result of a lack of price tags and price transparency. In the absence of clearly posted prices throughout the system (including at the wholesale level), participants resort to bartering and negotiation. After my doctor completed my treatment, his staff sent a bunch of medical billing codes and a reimbursement request to my insurance company. The insurance company very likely responded with an initial denial of the reimbursement request and/

or some of the billing codes. That is, the insurance company started off the negotiation with the most extreme initial bargaining position—it offered to pay nothing. There most likely followed a tortuous three-month negotiation over which billing codes would be approved and how much the doctor would get paid for each code. It's just like the slow and tedious negotiation process that you must undertake if you want to buy a blanket at a bazaar while you are on vacation in a foreign country.

That entire process can be eliminated with price tags, since price tags eliminate the need to negotiate back and forth over the final price (i.e., what the doctor will eventually be paid for his services). So, if you want to know where all the savings come from when you compare America's 17.9 percent of GDP spent on healthcare with Singapore's 4.2 percent, a major part of the answer is that you no longer need four full-time employees backing up a single provider of medical services. You no longer need massive numbers of insurance-billing employees to handle the back-and-forth price and reimbursement negotiations required by our current healthcare financing system.

I also should emphasize an additional benefit of price tags: justice. John Wanamaker, the inventor of the price tag, was a Quaker (i.e., a member of the Society of Friends, the Christian denomination). Quakers believe that all people are equal before God and that any Quaker doing business should therefore charge all his customers the same price for the same item. The price tag was a simple way of doing that. Any and all customers who were willing to pay the price displayed on a price tag could buy at that price, regardless of race, religion, age, or ability to haggle.

We could use that sort of justice in our healthcare system because, at present, there is no justice. Patients receiving identical treatments get billed wildly different amounts depending on what type of health insurance they have, whether they have health insurance at all, and on the basis of how the back-and-forth bartering negotiation between provider and insurance company goes. That process is unfair as well as inefficient. And it can be rectified—immediately—by price tags.

ADDING DEDUCTIBLE SECURITY TO HEALTH INSURANCE

I spent many chapters going over the gains in efficiency that happen when providers pair high-deductible health insurance with fully funded health savings accounts. The key trick to making that pairing work is that providers must "gift" the amount of the annual deductible into health savings accounts, because the large majority of the population lacks either the savings habits necessary to fill those accounts by themselves or the financial resources necessary to deposit sufficient amounts into those accounts.

Behavioral economists blame people's seeming inability to save enough on "decision-making myopia"—the tendency to focus on the here and now to the detriment of the future. People are prone to decision-making myopia because our ancestors had short life expectancies. It didn't make sense for them to plan for old age, or retirement, or healthcare needs many years in advance. Chances were, they wouldn't live long enough to benefit from higher present-day savings levels. We have a genetic legacy of focusing too much on the present and not saving enough for the future.

When it comes to retirement savings, we remedied that problem by creating Social Security as a mandatory savings program to overcome people's evolutionary reluctance to save enough for the future. To remedy that problem when it comes to healthcare savings, I recommend deductible security, or the policy already explained of having an insurance provider—a private company like Whole Foods Market or a government entity like the state of Indiana—gift the amount of the annual insurance deductible into people's health savings accounts. These deductible security gifts are a form of savings. But they are savings initiated by the provider rather than the individual.

My next policy recommendation is to have any company selling health insurance offer deductible security health insurance plans— that is, plans that pair a high-deductible health insurance policy with a health savings account into which the provider deposits the amount of the annual insurance deductible every year. Such a law is necessary because private insurance companies currently lack any incentive to market such plans. Why? Because deductible security health insurance plans slash healthcare spending by 35 percent, on average. That leads to a 35 percent reduction in insurance company profits. So it's no wonder that insurance companies have not actively marketed these plans, which benefit everyone but the insurance companies.

To overcome that hurdle, we must require that insurance companies offer and market these plans. I would go so far as to require that deductible security health insurance plans be the primary plans offered to providers—the ones that insurance companies *have* to pitch first and most aggressively to companies and governments wishing to offer health insurance to employees or entitlement recipients. Other health insurance plans could also be marketed, but only after full information is given about deductible security plans.

ENCOURAGING ADVANTAGEOUS SELECTION WITH AGE-RATED HEALTH INSURANCE

My final policy suggestion is for the United States to switch to age-rated—rather than community-rated—health insurance. Community rating was made mandatory by the Affordable Care Act. It involves placing everyone in a geographic area—typically a state— into the same insurance pool. As a result, everybody in the pool gets charged the same premium regardless of health status or preexisting conditions. The premium is the same for young and old, healthy and unhealthy, men and women. The problem with setting a single premium is that it prompts adverse selection—the tendency of an insurance pool to become dominated by the sickest and most costly as healthier people drop out, repelled by a pricing system that massively overcharges the healthy to pay for the care of the sick.

There is, of course, a compassionate and charitable point to doing that. Preexisting conditions are expensive, but many would want them funded in one way or another in order to provide good quality healthcare to those burdened with preexisting conditions. It's a matter of taking care of those in need. But adverse selection renders community-rated health insurance the wrong way to go about funding that charitable impulse. The very people you need to obtain surplus money from—the younger and healthier—are presented with intense financial incentives to exit the system altogether. What is needed is a system in which the young and healthy find it advantageous to participate and thus in which there will be enough money collected in premiums from the young and healthy to pay for the costs associated with the older and sicker.

Age-rated health insurance does this by creating insurance pools in which everybody—including, crucially, the healthiest—find it advantageous to pay premiums and participate on a voluntary basis. The trick is to create age bands that are not too wide. Singapore, for instance, has a band for twenty-one- to twenty-five-year-olds, followed by a band for twenty-five- to thirty-year-olds, followed by a band for thirty-one- to thirty-five-year-olds, and so on.

Because healthcare costs are, on average, very strongly positively correlated with age, each successive age group is charged a successively higher premium. But because the bands are so narrow in terms of age increments, there is not a huge difference within each group in terms of the average healthcare costs of the most and least sickly. Since everyone is about the same age, there is no need to massively over-charge the younger and healthier to pay for the older and sicker (as there is with community rating, which dumps everyone of all ages into the same insurance pool). The narrow age and spending gradient within each band allows insurance companies to set a single premium for each age band knowing that nearly everybody in that age group will find it fair—including the youngest and healthiest within each age band. The result is advantageous—rather than adverse—selection, as the insurance system can voluntarily retain the young and healthy.

Please note that while price tags and deductible security are already legal under the Affordable Care Act, we would need to over-turn the Affordable Care Act's community rating requirement if we were to proceed to age-rated health insurance. But given the Afford-able Care Act's failure to contain costs and deliver insurance coverage for all, as promised, the benefits of age-rated health insurance become even more obvious. The Affordable Care Act attempted to overcome the adverse selection generated by community rating by imposing fines and taxes on anyone without health insurance. But those disincentives were not strong enough to prevent adverse selection. The only alterna-tive is to switch to a system that encourages *advantageous* selection—something that age-rated health insurance does with aplomb.

Please understand that we already have two massive government-funded age-rated health insurance plans—Medicare and the Chil-dren's Health Insurance Program (CHIP). Medicare is for people age sixty-five and up. CHIP is for children living in poverty. What we need to do is to expand the age-rated logic of these systems to other age groups. My preference would be to pass legislation to uphold the Affordable Care Act's worthy goal of ensuring that all are insured, by migrating from community rating to age rating. That would switch us from adverse to advantageous selection and create an insurance system where everybody—including, crucially, the young and healthy—have a personal financial incentive to stay in the system and thus pay enough in premiums to help cover the costs of the elderly, the less healthy, and those burdened by preexisting conditions.

FINAL THOUGHTS

My recommendations could have been more numerous—for example, I would like to sever the link between employment and health insurance. But in this book, I have chosen to stick to policies that have already been proven to work here in the United States. If implemented nation-wide, they would slash costs, cover preexisting conditions, and insure everybody. The transition would likely take only a decade or so. And then, from that vantage point, we would be able to tackle other reforms, including severing the tie between employment and health insurance coverage.

So, to recap, we need three things. Price tags to foster competition and cost-cutting among providers. Deductible security health insurance to deliver financial security and provide a strong incentive to eliminate waste. And age-rated health insurance to eliminate the adverse selection problem that plagues community-rated health insurance. These three items have been shown to be extremely effective here in the United States. And so, I think it would be fair to characterize them as *The Cure that Works.*

It's important to remember what Yogi Berra said about distinguishing between what works in theory and what works in practice. My plan is based on what works in practice. So it is my great hope that—after appropriate debate and discussion—*The Cure that Works* can serve as the basis for reforming our healthcare system so that we no long deliver mediocre results at sky-high prices. The land that I love has always been able to reinvent itself for the better.

If we act now, high quality, low prices, and universal access are only a few years away.

Chapter 29

Help Defeat
the Special Interests

We need Singapore-style healthcare reform. Not only does Singapore deliver the world's best healthcare at the world's lowest costs; every major aspect of Singapore's system was originated in America and has been shown to work successfully right here in the United States. So reform is possible not only in theory, but also in practice.

There is one huge obstacle, though: special interests.

Insurance companies, pharmaceutical giants, massive hospital chains, medical device makers, and other healthcare special interests spend hundreds of millions of dollars per year lobbying the government for favors. They ask for—*and get!*—tax breaks, subsidies, loan guarantees, exemptions from labor laws, and, most importantly, exemptions from competition.

The amount of money they devote to manipulating our government is staggering. Indeed, it is a little-known fact that healthcare special interests spend more on lobbying than anyone else, including Wall Street and the defense industry. Table 29.1 tells the tale. It ranks US industries by how much money they each spent on lobbying the federal government between 1998 and 2018; the top twenty are shown. *Both* of the top spots, as well as five of the top twenty, are occupied by healthcare special interests.

29.1 The Twenty Industries with the Highest Federal Lobbying Expenditures between 1998 and 2018[1]

Rank	Industry	Total
1	Pharmaceuticals/Health Products	$3,937,356,877
2	Insurance	2,704,636,807
3	Electric Utilities	2,353,570,360
4	Electronics Mfg & Equip	2,230,043,875
5	Business Associations	2,217,425,929
6	Oil & Gas	2,096,923,653
7	Misc Manufacturing & Distributing	1,687,618,725
8	Education	1,633,122,450
9	Hospitals/Nursing Homes	1,604,696,566
10	Securities & Investment	1,548,537,463
11	Telecom Services	1,538,038,434
12	Real Estate	1,522,817,733
13	Health Professionals	1,453,558,737
14	Civil Servants/Public Officials	1,437,730,535
15	Air Transport	1,392,972,584
16	Health Services/HMOs	1,108,096,260
17	Defense Aerospace	1,101,303,893
18	Automotive	1,093,277,816
19	Misc Issues	1,056,530,748
20	TV/Movies/Music	1,035,372,905

Source: The Center for Responsive Politics, http://OpenSecrets.org.

As you might expect, the #1 position in Table 29.1 is held by the pharmaceuticals/health products industry, which spent $3.9 billion lobbying the government between 1998 and 2018. Within this industry, the biggest spenders on lobbying include the Pharmaceuticals Research & Manufacturers of America, the Biotechnology Innovation Organization, and "Big Pharma" drug makers such as Pfizer, Amgen, and Novartis.

Position #2 is occupied by the insurance industry, which spent $2.7 billion on lobbying efforts over those twenty years. The largest spenders within the insurance industry include the American Council of Life Insurers, America's Health Insurance Plans, BlueCross BlueShield, and any number of prominent insurance companies, such as Prudential Financial, MetLife, State Farm, and Aflac.

Position #9 is held by the hospitals/nursing homes industry. Its members spent a combined total of $1.6 billion lobbying the federal government between 1998 and 2018. The top spenders in this industry include the American Hospital Association, the American Health Care Association, the Federation of American Hospitals, and major for-profit hospital groups like Encompass Health, Kindred Healthcare, and Select Medical Corporation.

Position #13 is held by health professionals, who together spent a combined $1.5 billion on lobbying between 1998 and 2018. Their biggest spenders include the American Medical Association, the American Academy of Family Physicians, the American Nurses Association, the American Congress of Obstetricians & Gynecologists, and the American Academy of Orthopaedic Surgeons.

Position #16 is occupied by the health services/HMOs industry. Its members spent a combined $1.1 billion lobbying the government between 1998 and 2018. The industry's biggest spenders include UnitedHealth Group, Kaiser Permanente, DaVita Healthcare Partners, Humana, Aetna, and BlueCross BlueShield (whose $1.5 million of lobbying money spent on behalf of the health services/HMOs industry is separate from the $3.3 million it spent lobbying for the pharmaceuticals/health products industry over the same period).

The five healthcare industry groups in Table 29.1 spent a combined total of $10.8 billion lobbying the government between 1998 and 2018. According to OpenSecrets.org, that was 19.6 percent of the $55.1 billion spent on lobbying by *all* industry groups in the United States over that time period.

So when we consider what it will take to achieve Singapore-style healthcare reform, we must take into account the massive power and influence of the special interests that have spent decades lobbying the government and cultivating relationships. Anybody advocating for Singapore-style healthcare reform will face well organized and highly connected special interest groups with massive financial resources at their disposal.

I am hopeful that many will join us as allies. But others will consider Singapore-style reform to be too large a threat to their profits and their power. They will, of course, lobby the government as they have always done, hoping to preserve their profits and their perks. But they will also be tempted to go on the attack to try to discredit or besmirch anyone who supports Singapore-style healthcare reform.

Milder tactics may include accusing the backers of Singapore-style reform of being wild-eyed idealists or uninformed amateurs who don't know anything about how healthcare "really" works. Stronger tactics may include accusing Singapore-style reform advocates of wanting to destroy our social safety net. Singapore advocates will very likely be accused of wanting to gut Medicaid and Medicare, of trying to establish a totally capitalist medical system that only cares about profits and wanting to create massive inequalities between the quality of healthcare delivered to the poor and the rich.

Any such accusations will, of course, be outright lies. Singapore delivers not only the world's best healthcare at the lowest cost, but also the *same* healthcare to all its citizens, rich and poor alike.

Those facts are more than enough to draw ordinary Americans together in support of Singapore-style healthcare reform. But there is too much money at stake for many of the current incumbents to step aside politely. They will fight, and they will fight dirty.

For that reason, I feel that the only way to guarantee success for Singapore-style healthcare reform is to enlist millions of my fellow Americans in a truly grassroots reform movement. If we work together to put pressure on Congress and the president, on governors and legislatures, on influential newspapers and magazines, we will be able to break the power of the incumbent special interests.

But how can we do that? There is only one way: political and social organizing.

We are lucky to live in the age of the internet. Ordinary people can communicate directly to each other and to their political representatives conveniently and at low cost through email, Facebook, Twitter, Pinterest, YouTube, Instagram, podcasts, blogs, webpages, and even text messages. We can use these tools to organize and coordinate. We can construct an unstoppably powerful grassroots social movement—one that will be able to force the changes necessary to replace our hideously expensive and mediocre healthcare system with one that provides financial and medical security for the poor while also forcing competition and efficiency upon healthcare providers.

Working together, we can overcome special interest lobbying.

Working together, we can restore hope and security to the most vulnerable.

Working together, we can save trillions of dollars and millions of lives.

So please work with us to deliver the healthcare that Americans both want and deserve.

Appendix I

Why Doesn't Anybody Know about Singapore's Healthcare System?

Very few people know about Singapore's remarkable healthcare system. One major reason for that ignorance is simply a lack of available data. The World Health Organization (WHO) publishes healthcare data for every nation in the world, but their data retrieval system is so cumbersome and confusing that anyone trying to use it for the first time will likely quit before getting very far. By contrast, the healthcare data collected and disseminated by the Organization for Economic Cooperation and Development (OECD) is simple and easy to navigate. The OECD's data site also produces a plethora of premade charts and graphs. Consequently, it's only natural that journalists tend to rely on the OECD's data when comparing different countries' healthcare systems.

Unfortunately, by relying on the OECD's healthcare data, people consistently overlook Singapore. As previously mentioned, the OECD is a private club of thirty-four nations. As you might expect of an influential international organization, it includes major economic powers, such as the United States, Germany, and China. But it also includes a bunch of really small countries, such as Estonia, Luxembourg, Slovenia, and, yes, Iceland. Singapore, though, is not a member. So when journalists and academics rely on only the OECD's healthcare data, they end up missing Singapore and its world-class performance.

Another reason very few people know about Singapore's healthcare system is the way that the debate over healthcare policy has been framed here in the United States. Ever since Medicare and Medicaid were enacted back in 1965, any subsequent debate about expanding or modifying those programs has repeatedly revolved around comparing how well they work (or don't work) against the national healthcare systems of just a handful of countries—most prominently Canada and the United Kingdom. Again, Singapore is ignored—this time because it wasn't one of the standard comparison countries back when the comparisons started being made in the 1960s.

The same has been true regarding the related debate over whether the United States should establish a single-payer national healthcare system funded entirely by the government. Analysts and pundits have focused almost exclusively on comparing the US healthcare system with the healthcare systems of countries like Canada and the United Kingdom, which have single-payer systems. Because Singapore doesn't have a single-payer system, it has been overlooked yet again.

Singapore's success has also been easy to overlook because Singapore's healthcare system didn't take on its current configuration until the early 1990s. Thus, the superiority of Singapore's healthcare system wasn't yet proved when First Lady Hillary Clinton headed up her husband's Task Force on National Health Care Reform in 1993. There was only about fifteen years' worth of data by the time the battle over the Affordable Care Act got really heated in 2009. During the debate, a few isolated pundits and newspaper columnists *did* suggest Singapore as an alternative. But nobody with any major political influence advocated for wholesale, root-and-branch reform based on Singapore's success.

Instead, the debate revolved almost entirely around how to keep America's wasteful third-party system in place while tacking on universal coverage through personal and employer mandates. Unfortunately, the final version of the Affordable Care Act left in place all the bad incentives that already existed with regard to third-party payments. Forty million Americans stood to gain insurance coverage—but with the same bad incentives as the other 270 million who already had insurance. As a result, all 310 million would have to continue living with sky-high prices and mediocre outcomes. Instead of fixing a universally bad system, Congress voted to make our bad system universally available.

Sadly, our policy elites still don't know much about Singapore's healthcare system. The most widely read report comparing international healthcare systems is the Commonwealth Fund's annually updated publication, *International Profiles of Health Care Systems*. The update published in 2014 had dossiers comparing the healthcare systems of fourteen countries. It's a great report, but the fourteen countries are Australia, Canada, Denmark, England, France, Germany, Italy, Japan, the Netherlands, New Zealand, Norway, Sweden, Switzerland, and the United States. Singapore was not included until the 2015 update. And because it wasn't, anybody looking through that report in any previous year would have missed the country that *actually has* the world's best healthcare system.

In closing, I should point out one additional reason why Singapore's healthcare system has been overlooked. Unlike the other reasons, it has to do with a factor internal to Singapore, namely the diligence with which the government of Singapore has combed the world for good ideas. If you walk around one of Singapore's hospitals, the staff will explain that they borrowed or adapted almost *all* of their good ideas—that *this* charting design came from the Mayo Clinic; that they copied *that* part of their medical records system from the United Kingdom; that they modeled *this* eldercare facility on a design that they happened to come across in Osaka.

Singapore's Ministry of Health has systematically scoured the world to determine "best practice" in every aspect of healthcare delivery. It sends out fact-finding missions and pays for Singapore's best students to study medicine and public health at top foreign universities—places like Harvard, Oxford, Tokyo University, Johns Hopkins, Stanford, the University of Sydney, and the Sorbonne. Those professionals come back a few years later having seen every sort of healthcare system. They can then exchange ideas and make informed judgments about what works best.

Put another way, nearly all the intellectual traffic between Singapore and the rest of the world has consisted of Singaporeans going abroad rather than foreigners coming to visit Singapore. As a result, Singapore's success in implementing the best ideas from around the world has gone largely unnoticed.

Reductions in Government Healthcare Spending under Singapore's System of Healthcare Financing

Singapore's healthcare-financing system takes pressure off the government's general budget in two ways. The first is more obvious: the billions of dollars that have been saved thanks to MediSave and MediFund can help to pay for a substantial fraction of Singapore's annual healthcare expenditures, without the government having to spend a single cent of current tax revenues. The second way is less obvious: the government can purchase healthcare services for the poor at extremely low prices. Because of the high degree of competition facilitated by consumers seeking to maximize health while preserving their health savings, there are incredibly low healthcare prices for *everybody*. So when the government of Singapore uses current tax revenues to provide direct subsidies, it can do so within the world's highest-quality, lowest-cost healthcare system and thereby purchase a lot of healthcare at extremely low prices.

The natural result is that Singapore's government spends less than any other developed government on healthcare. This is made clear by Figure A.1, which shows how much Singapore and the high-income OECD nations are each spending on healthcare as a fraction of their respective GDPs. The figure arranges the countries in order, from most to least public spending on healthcare. At the top is the Netherlands, whose government spends 10.1 percent of its GDP on publicly provided healthcare. Then, in sequence, Denmark, France, Germany, Japan, Austria, New Zealand, Belgium and the United States all spend at least 8 percent of GDP on publicly funded healthcare. The remaining twenty-five countries continue in order down the figure, with Singapore coming in at just 1.5 percent of GDP. That's less than half of the 3.1 percent being spent by the lowest-spending OECD country, Mexico. It's also 75 percent less than the OECD average of 6.7 percent of GDP, 81 percent less than the 8.0 percent of GDP being spent by the United States, and 85 percent less than the 10.1 percent of GDP being spent by the Netherlands.

So if somebody asks you to list the benefits of Singapore's 3Ms system of automatic healthcare savings and competition among service providers, don't just point out the high quality and low costs enjoyed by individuals. Also point out how much money the system saves the government and, implicitly, how much money is thereby freed up to be spent on other things, such as better schools, a stronger national defense, or better infrastructure.

Some of the savings can also be directed toward funding public health initiatives. This is important because so much of government healthcare spending in the United States ends up being directed toward taking care of people who are already ill—something that cynics refer to as "sickcare" (as opposed to "healthcare"). And because public health advances have accounted for so many of the improvements in quality of life and longevity in the twentieth century, funding public health initiatives becomes all the more desirable.

Figure A.1: Public Healthcare Expenditures as a Percentage of GDP for Each of the Thirty-Four OECD Nations Plus Singapore

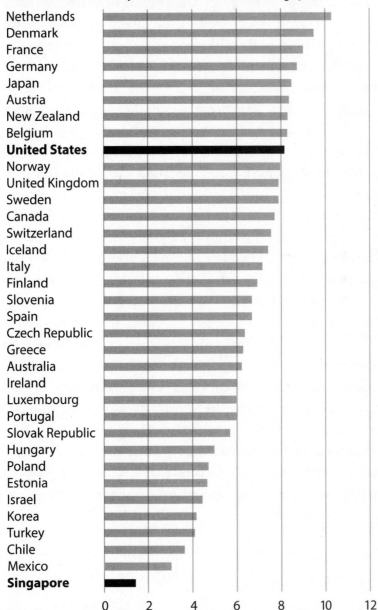

Sources: OECD Health Data 2014, Organization for Economic Cooperation and Development (OECD), http://data. oecd.org. Health, Nutrition, and Health Statistics (available online at World DataBank, The World Bank), https:// datacatalog.worldbank.org.

Singapore goes to great lengths to promote preventive public health efforts that help keep people from getting sick in the first place. In addition to public health spending on disease abatement, clean water, and environmental health, the Singaporean government provides reduced-cost preventive care to the poor and indigent through a variety of programs, including school-based dental clinics, senior care centers, preventive screening programs (like BreastScreen Singapore), publicly-funded gyms in every neighborhood, green belts for outdoor exercise throughout the country, and neighborhood markets that sell affordable, healthy food, especially inexpensive fruits and vegetables.

The government also uses general tax revenues to maintain a wide variety of subsidy programs that pay for preventive and rehabilitation services not already delivered free of charge. These include the Community Health Assistance Scheme, the Marriage and Parenthood Scheme, the Interim Disability Assistance Programme for the Elderly, and the large grants that the government gives to voluntary welfare organizations to help cover the costs of running everything from community hospitals to meals-on-wheels programs.

In each case, the government's efforts are assisted by the fact that the 3Ms and competition have freed up so much of the government's budget from having to pay for healthcare. If we want that flexibility too, then we'll need to implement health savings accounts for first parties and competition among second parties. Only by empowering first parties as comparison shoppers can government expenditures on healthcare be cut so low.

Acknowledgments

Every book has a thousand indirect contributors, each bestowing an idea, insight, or inspiration. Their names must remain unsung, for the author feels their influence but knows not their names. To each of them, though, let me express deep thanks and admiration.

Every book also has dozens of direct contributors, well-known to the author. These should be thanked liberally and publicly. To that end, let me begin with my good friend Debbie Freund, who gave extensive early feedback and opened many doors for me. Deborah Mashek also provided extensive early suggestions that helped to ensure that the book would be clear and intuitive for readers new to healthcare policy.

Jay Kempton and Dr. Keith Smith cannot be thanked enough for starting the Free Market Medical Association here in the United States. Their work in the private sector has complemented the healthcare reform efforts of Seema Verma, Mike Pence, and Mitch Daniels in the public sector.

I am deeply indebted to Mei Lin Fung for shepherding me around Singapore so that I could study its awe-inspiring healthcare system. Many thanks to the experts, providers, and policymakers I met there, including Kelvin Bryan Tan, Kai Hong Phua, Jeremy Lim, Joel Loh, Bee Lian Ang, Ching Yee Tan, Kee Seng Chia, and Teng Lit Liat.

I have been very lucky that so many people have helped to promote my healthcare reform ideas. They include David Butze, Richard Schiffrin, Luis Buhler, Marc Chazaud, Mary Hart, Burt Sugarman, Bat Masterson, Kurt Henry, Joe Henehan, Susan Henehan, Warner Henry, Devo Anderson, Ahmed Calvo, Kari Anderson, Charles Munger Jr., Vidar Jorgensen, Jim Blew, Pete Weber, Julian Morris, Fred Balitzer, Rod Wilson, Charles Kessler, Carla Tully, Jeff Harris, Paul and Lori Zak, Janice Rutherford, Avik Roy, Tevi Troy, Lan Hee Chen, George Schultz, John Cogan, David Spady, Boo H. Kwa, Anna Cable, Kurt Henry, John Levy, Brooke Allen, Dan Cardell, Harris Koenig, Carl Dameron, Igor Konfisakhar, John Puzder, Andrew Puzder, Ken Weinstein, Joaquin Arambula, Jeffrey Anderson, Matthew Hunter, Avik Roy, Larry Carr, Don Gould, Patricia Horoho, Jodi Carrol, Bat Masterson, Richard Relph, Grover Norquist, Julian Morris, Mike Jones, Steve PonTell, Gerry Smedinghoff, Linda Roghaar, Matt Krisiloff, Charles Green, Sam Altman, Erin Friedman, Mark Zitter, Sally Pipes, Paul DeMuro, Wade Ren, Maggie Tsai, Michael Ross, Scott Atlas, Rich Phillips, Joseph Szokol, Marquerite Manela, Robert Reischauer, Deborah Kekone, Williamson Evers, Joe Lonsdale, Julie and Jerry Biggs, Richard Malott, James Ortiz, Mark Fesen, Dale Broome, Tom Edmonds, Susan Broome, Cristina Valle Parke, Travis Parke, Mark Skousen, Tom Campbell, Ray and Fern Musser, John Mackey, Harvey and Karen Cohen, Glenn Noreen, Phil Paule, and John Goodman, the economist who invented health savings accounts and who has fought for decades to reform our failing healthcare system. John deserves a Presidential Medal of Freedom.

I am grateful to Laureen Cantwell and Neva Friedenn for copy-editing the first draft and to Ben Levine for shopping it around to publishing houses. Gary Newman also deserves many plaudits for designing the look and feel of the graphs and figures used in this book.

I would like to thank Regnery Publishing's Marji Ross, Anne Mulrooney, Timothy Meads, Harry Crocker, and Kathleen Curran for ensuring a lucid and appealing final product. Any errors or omissions are mine.

And, finally, I would like to thank my two favorite physicians: my mom, Dr. Mikiko Flynn, and my bride, Dr. Rupali Chadha Flynn.

Notes

Introduction

1. The exact figure is 17.9 percent. "National Health Expenditure Projections 2017-26," Office of the Actuary, Centers for Medicare and Medicaid Services, February 14, 2018.
2. Economic Report of the President, US Government Publishing Office (GPO), and "The 2018 Annual Report of the Board of Trustees of the Federal Old-Age and Survivors Insurance and Federal Disability Insurance Trust Funds," Old Age, Survivors, and Disability Trust Fund Trustees' Report. NB: The official government name for Social Security is the Old Age, Survivors, and Disability Trust Fund.

Chapter 1: The Cabbie's Tale

1. CIA World Factbook, 2018, Central Intelligence Agency.
2. Author calculations based on data from the "CIA World Factbook," 2018, Central Intelligence Agency.
3. The Bloomberg Healthiest Country rankings and underlying methodology is available at: https://web.archive.org/

web/20120907044847/http://images.businessweek.com/
bloomberg/pdfs/WORLDS_HEALTHIEST_COUNTRIES.
pdf.

Chapter 2: Singapore Past and Present

1. "Singapore is the Greenest City in Asia, according to New
    Survey," February 17, 2011, E360 Digest, Environment 360,
    Yale School of Forestry and Environmental Studies; Tim
    Nelson, "MIT Uses Algorithms to Find the World's Greenest
    Cities," January 23, 2018, *Architectural Digest*.
2. See Boston Consulting Group, 2014, "Global Wealth 2014:
    Riding a Wave of Growth," BCG Perspectives, and previous
    reports for 2012 and 2011, https://www.bcgperspectives.com/
    content/articles/financial_institutions_business_unit_strategy_
    global_wealth_2014_riding_wave_growth/.
3. Program for International Student Assessment, http://www.
    oecd.org/pisa/. The Learning Curve results are published by
    Pearson: https://web.archive.org/web/20141231040513/http://
    thelearningcurve.pearson.com/reports/the-learning-curve-
    report-2014.
4. Direct communication with Singapore's Ministry of Education.
5. The Condition of Education 2014, National Center for
    Education Statistics, US Department of Education.
6. In recent decades, Singapore's employee and employer
    contributions were both reduced. Today, they stand at a
    combined total of 36 percent—20 percent from the employee
    and 16 percent from the employer. But that lower individual
    savings rate of 36 percent is still much higher than anything the
    United States, Western Europe, or Japan has accomplished. I
    should also mention that the government guarantees individuals
    a minimum 2.5 percent per year rate of return on CPF savings
    balances—so you can understand why the policy remains
    widely popular.
7. OECD Tax Database, The Tax Foundation.

Chapter 3: Singapore's Healthcare Supremacy

1. World Bank Open Data, The World Bank, https://data. worldbank.org.
2. The Bloomberg Healthiest Country rankings and underlying methodology is available at: https://web.archive.org/ web/20120907044847/http://images.businessweek.com/ bloomberg/pdfs/WORLDS_HEALTHIEST_COUNTRIES. pdf.
3. These figures should also make you skeptical whenever you come across a headline along the lines of, "America's Nursing Shortage Critical" or "America's Imminent Doctor Shortage." If we used doctors and nurses as efficiently as Singapore does, we wouldn't need nearly as many doctors and nurses. "Shortage" solved. Becoming more efficient would also fit in nicely with the fact that one-third of US physicians are expected to retire in the next ten years (Association of American Medical Colleges, 2017). That exodus means that we could switch over to Singaporean levels of medical efficiency without causing massive unemployment problems for currently practicing MDs. The same would be true for nurses, who now average fifty years of age and are thus set to retire in massive numbers over the next fifteen years (National Nursing Workforce Study, National Council of State Boards of Nursing, 2017).

Chapter 5: What We Could Do If We Copied Singapore

1. *The World Factbook* 2018, (Washington, D.C.: Central Intelligence Agency, 2018), https://www.cia.gov/library/ publications/the-world-factbook/index.html.
2. Social Security Administration, "The 2018 Annual Report of the Board of Trustees of the Federal Old-Age and Survivors Insurance and Federal Disability Insurance Trust Funds," https://www.ssa.gov/oact/TR/2018/tr2018.pdf.

Chapter 6: Why Is the US Healthcare System Doing So Badly?

1. Hoveround Personal Mobility Solutions, https://www. hoveround.com/home/more-information/.
2. And I do mean "only a few weeks," because my dad would have been the only person to ever use the machine. That's because it is illegal to sell the machine to another person who could then get more use out of it. That may puzzle you, but it is an unfortunate fact that US government regulations prohibit the resale of most medical devices; you can't buy a used one from a current owner to save money and you can't resell a used one to anyone but a licensed reseller, who is then only supposed to sell it if it is "recertified." The rule is supposed to protect the public from being subjected to older devices that no longer work well or from using the devices without proper medical supervision and guidance, but it ends up forcing everyone to purchase costly new devices or "certified pre-owned" devices, even in situations where older devices (such as a used Hoveround) wouldn't be a threat to anybody's health. That lack of choice creates monopoly power for medical device-makers, because their new products don't have to compete with used products on the open market. To see what a difference that makes in terms of prices and profits, imagine if used car sales were banned and people could only buy new cars. That prohibition would massively increase the price of new cars, because new cars would no longer have to compete with used cars for customers and sales.
3. T.A. Brennan, C.M. DesRoches, M.M. Mello, J. Peugh, W.M. Sage, D.M. Studdert, and K. Zapert, "Defensive medicine among high-risk specialist physicians in a volatile malpractice environment," *Journal of the American Medical Association* 293, no. 21 (2005): 2609–2617.
4. Jackson Healthcare, "Physician Study: Quantifying the Cost of Defensive Medicine," February 2010, http://www. jacksonhealthcare.com/media-room/surveys/defensive-medicine-study-2010/.

5. If true competition existed among insurance companies, this wouldn't be a problem. Low-cost innovators would come in and undercut the high premiums charged by incumbents. Unfortunately, true competition is lacking, since there are very few insurers due to a heavy regulatory regime that favors incumbents and stymies innovators. With so little competition, the insurance companies' easiest path to higher profits is not cost cutting but raising premiums, prices, and claims throughout the system.

Chapter 7: Provoking Profligacy with Low Out-Of-Pocket Costs

1. Out-of-pocket spending includes any payments made by first parties out of their own money and includes spending for insurance deductibles as well as copays (coinsurance) for prescriptions and procedures. As an example, imagine a patient with a 10 percent insurance copay rate. If his doctor writes him a prescription that costs a hundred dollars, his out-of-pocket spending would be ten dollars , with the other ninety dollars being picked up by his insurance company.
2. We're a mess when compared with all countries, rich *and* poor. If you look across all nations, only seven have smaller numbers for the fraction of private healthcare spending that comes out of pocket—Kiribati, Haiti, Mozambique, Botswana, South Africa, Timor-Leste, and Namibia.

Chapter 8: How "Single-Payer" Systems Spend Less Than We Do

1. At the time I wrote this sentence in late 2018, £30,000 was equal to about $40,000 in US currency.

Chapter 9: Empowering Prudence with First-Party Payments

1. To see where the 24 percent decline in real prices comes from, begin by noting that $100 of cosmetic surgery in 1992 would have cost $127 in 2013, due to the 27 percent increase in nominal cosmetic surgery prices. In the same way, $100 of general consumer goods in 1992 would have cost $167 in 2013

due to the 67 percent increase in the consumer price index. We can now compare the $127 for cosmetic surgery in 2013 with the $167 for overall consumer goods and see that cosmetic surgery was, relatively speaking, about 24 percent cheaper (i.e., $127 is about 24 percent less than $167.)

2. "Ten-Year Results on Radial Keratotomy Released," October 13, 1994, press release, National Eye Institute, National Institutes of Health, https://nei.nih.gov/news/pressreleases/ perkpressrelease.

3. Liz Segre, "LASIK Eye Surgery Cost," August 20, 2018, http:// www.allaboutvision.com/visionsurgery/cost.htm.

Chapter 10: The Origins of America's Employment-Based Health Insurance System

1. Henry J. Kaiser Family Foundation, 2018 Employer Health Benefits Survey, October 3, 2018, https://www.kff.org/health-costs/report/2018-employer-health-benefits-survey/.

2. The government also heavily promoted the sale of war bonds, since each bond sold meant less cash in circulation and thus a smaller likelihood of inflation.

Chapter 11: How to Engineer Low-Cost Health Insurance

1. As I will explain in later chapters, Singapore very intentionally avoided first-dollar coverage for its government-sponsored health insurance plan (MediShield), because first-dollar coverage causes so much harm via poor incentives and massively higher claims-processing costs.

2. Singapore's healthcare system also bans first-dollar coverage and does not allow everything to be covered by insurance policies. That probity mitigates moral hazard and the tendency for insurance to promote overconsumption.

Chapter 12: Visiting Singapore's Hospitals and Clinics

1. According to Ministry of Health data, the median wait time at polyclinics in August 2018 was twelve minutes in total,

comprised of two initial minutes from walking through the
door to completing registration, and then another ten minutes
until being seen by a doctor or a nurse. Median wait times to
see a doctor or nurse in Singapore's various public hospital
emergency rooms are not published regularly by the Ministry
of Health, but were reported by Minister for Health Gan Kim
Yong during parliamentary questions in 2013. He reported that
they ranged between fifteen and twenty-nine minutes in 2012.
(See "A&E patients prioritized, attended to based on severity of
conditions: Gan Kim Yong," by Vimita Mohandas, July 8,
2013, News 5 Tonight, Channel NewsAsia, http://www.
channelnewsasia.com/news/specialreports/parliament/news/a-
e-patients-prioritised/738108.html).
Patient satisfaction is higher at Singapore's public hospitals
than at US hospitals. While only 71 percent of US hospital
patients would recommend the hospital they were treated at,
fully 78 percent of Singapore's public hospital patients would
do so. That is especially surprising because the US data
includes both public and private hospitals, whereas the
Singapore data only includes public hospitals. (For the source
of the US hospital-recommendation statistic, which was based
on surveys of patients at 4,143 US hospitals, see the "April
2015 Public Report: July 2013–June 2014 discharges,"
published by Hospital Consumer Assessment of Healthcare
Providers and Systems [HCAHPS], https://www.hcahpsonline.
org/globalassets/hcahps/summary-analyses/summary-results/
april-2015-public-report-july-2013-june-2014-discharges.pdf.
For the source of the Singapore hospital-recommendation
statistic, which was based on patients surveyed at Singapore's
seven public hospitals, see "Patient Satisfaction Survey 2013,"
which was published by the Singapore Ministry of Health as
Annex A to the July 10, 2014 press release titled, "More
Healthcare Institutions Have Met the Expectations of Patients
in 2013 Patient Satisfaction Survey," https://www.moh.gov.sg/
content/moh_web/home/pressRoom/

pressRoomItemRelease/2014/more-healthcare-institutions-
have-met-the-expectations-of-patien.html.)

2. Shen, Yugeng and Lee, Lin Hui, "Improving the wait time until
   consultation at the emergency department," January 3, 2018,
   BMJ Open Quality, 7(1): e000131. doi: 10.1136/bmjoq-2017-
   000131.

3. These grants are separate from and in addition to any "direct
   subsidy" money that the government may be directing to the
   hospital to cover the medical bills of indigent (subsidized)
   patients. See Chapter 16 for details.

4. When you fly into Singapore and are approaching customs at
   Changi International Airport, you will see many giant signs
   that read, "WARNING: DEATH FOR DRUG
   TRAFFICKERS UNDER SINGAPORE LAW." And they
   mean it. Even the smallest amount of cocaine, heroin, or meth
   will get you a death sentence.

Chapter 13: MediSave and the Miraculous 3Ms

1. If you feel dumb following the advice of a Yankee catcher best
   known for striking out on syntax, please know that Albert
   Einstein is said to have agreed with Yogi Berra: "In theory,
   theory and practice are the same. In practice, they are not."

2. As I will discuss more in a later chapter, the Ministry of Health
   has intentionally placed the doctors and nurses at public
   hospitals on fixed annual salaries. Thus, they get paid exactly
   the same whether they are treating poorer patients or richer
   patients. This helps ensure that the poor receive exactly the
   same level of care as the rich, as there is zero financial incentive
   to do more for the richer patients or spend more time with
   them.

3. A cynic might argue that the Social Security "lock box" is not
   meant to guard the contents *for* you—it's meant to guard the
   contents *from* you.

4. At 2018 exchange rates, one Singapore dollar equaled 73 cents
   worth of US money (i.e., S$1.00 = $0.80). So, the S$3,000

deposited into each child's MediSave Account is worth about $2,190 in US money.

5. Department of Statistics Singapore, https://www.singstat.gov.sg/find-data/search-by-theme/households/households/latest-data.

6. US Census Bureau, https://www.census.gov/housing/hvs/files/currenthvspress.pdf.

7. Board of Governors of the Federal Reserve System, "Report on the Economic Well-Being of U.S. Households in 2017," May 2018, https://www.federalreserve.gov/publications/files/2017-report-economic-well-being-us-households-201805.pdf.

8. Ministry of Health, "Medisave Accounts and Balances, Annual," https://data.gov.sg/dataset/medisave-accounts-and-balances-annual.

Chapter 14: MediShield and the Right Incentives

1. As I will discuss later, pre-2015 MediShield was an "opt-out" program, meaning that every citizen and permanent resident was automatically enrolled and "defaulted into" the program. They would then stay enrolled permanently, unless they went out of their way to sign a document indicating their desire to opt out of the program. Those opting out were essentially choosing either to self-insure or to rely exclusively on employer-sponsored health benefits. While there is no published data on the demographics of those opting out of MediShield, the common supposition is that they were probably high earners with very good employer-sponsored health benefits. By contrast, MediShield's extremely low premiums were very attractive to the poor, who were unlikely to be able to self-insure or have access to generous employer-sponsored health benefits. So it is presumed that poorer Singaporeans almost never elected to opt out of MediShield. Those speculations and suppositions were made moot in 2015, however, when the expanded and renamed MediShield Life health insurance

program made participation by citizens and permanent residents mandatory. See Chapter 20 for the details.

2. Your humble author can report on a very unlikely pedestrian accident. I was hit by a valet parking attendant with my own car. Yes, my own car. He popped the clutch while I was walking in front of the vehicle. My advice: buy lots of insurance.

3. After one of my lectures on Singapore's healthcare system, a former hospital administrator came up to talk to me. He had previously run three hospitals in the Denver area. He told me that his hospitals had, on multiple occasions, sent heart bypass patients to either Thailand or Singapore for surgery. He said that even after including round-trip, first-class plane tickets and paying for a week or two recuperating overseas, sending them overseas was still *less than half as costly* as doing the surgeries in Denver.

Chapter 15: MediShield Encourages Participation and Fairness with Age-Rated Insurance

1. Current Population Survey, 2011, US Census Bureau.
2. Larry DeWitt, "Research Note #3: Details of Ida May Fuller's Payroll Tax Contributions," Research Notes and Special Studies by the Historian's Office, July 1996, United States Social Security Administration, https://www.ssa.gov/history/idapayroll.html.

Chapter 16: MediFund and Direct Subsidies: Singapore's Amazing Healthcare Safety Net

1. "FY2017 Budget Statement," 2017, government of Singapore, https://www.singaporebudget.gov.sg/data/budget_2017/download/FY2017_Budget_Statement.pdf.
2. Jeremy Lim, *Myth or Magic: The Singapore Healthcare System.* (Singapore: Select Publishing, 2013).
3. Ibid.

4. Statistics on the rate of approval are not published on a regular basis by the Medical Endowment Fund. However, the approval rate has been stated as 99.7 percent by a minister for health when answering questions in Parliament. See Balaji Sadasivan, "Public Sector Hospitals (Fee increases)," *Singapore Parliament Reports, Hansard,* October 1, 2002. For the percent of applicants receiving full assistance see *Medical Endowment Scheme Annual Report 2013/2014,* posted online by the Singapore Ministry of Health.

5. Author's calculation. Singapore's GDP in 2014 was S$394.751 billion (SingStats, singstat.gov.sg). Singapore's 2014 healthcare spending was 4.9 percent of that amount, or S$19.342 billion (World Health Organization, Global Health Observatory, who.int/gho/en). So that year's MediFund disbursements of S$157.5 million ("Medifund Applications and Grants Distributed, Annual," data.gov.singapore) represented 0.8 percent of Singapore's 2014 healthcare spending.

6. "The financial hole for Social Security and Medicare is even deeper than the experts say," by James C. Capretta, Market Watch, June 16, 2018, https://www.marketwatch.com/story/the-financial-hole-for-social-security-and-medicare-is-even-deeper-than-the-experts-say-2018-06-15.

7. Ibid.

Chapter 17: Singapore's Multiple Ward Classes: Healthcare, Not Hotels

1. But not always. I was amused to hear that many older Singaporeans opted for B2 and C class wards even if they were extremely wealthy. They grew up without air conditioning and hate it. So, they are more than happy to stay six or nine to a room if it means that they can rest and recuperate without cold air blowing on them.

Chapter 18: Pharmaceuticals in Singapore

1. Sam Peltzman, "An Evaluation of Consumer Protection Legislation: The 1962 Drug Amendments," *Journal of Political Economy* 81 no. 5 (1973): 1051.
2. Khaw Boon Wan, Singapore Parliament Reports (Hansard), March 4, 2011.

CHAPTER 20: MediShield Life and the Future of Singapore's Healthcare System

1. As noted in an earlier chapter, about 6 percent of the population did opt out of MediShield, either because they felt comfortable self-insuring or because they preferred to rely exclusively on the private health insurance coverage provided by their employers.
2. They would wait to see if their house burned down and only sign up for fire insurance if it did. After obtaining an insurance policy, they would then immediately file a claim and ask for their house to be rebuilt despite never having paid a single monthly premium into the fire insurance system.

Chapter 21: The State of Indiana's Consumer-Driven Healthcare Plan

1. Consumer-directed healthcare plans, CDHPs, are sometimes alternatively classified as high deductible healthcare plans with savings option, or HDHP/SOs.
2. Henry J. Kaiser Family Foundation, "2018 Employer Health Benefits Survey," October 3 2018, https://www.kff.org/health-costs/report/2018-employer-health-benefits-survey/.
3. Ibid.
4. Ibid.
5. Aetna Health Fund, "Eighth Annual Aetna Health Fund Study: Health Fund Consumer-Directed Plans Continue to Reduce Health Care Costs for Employers: Plans also encourage members to take a more active role in their health," 2011.

6. Employee Benefit Research Institute, "Findings from the 2011 EBRI/MGA Consumer Engagement in Health Care Survey," EBRI Issue Brief No. 365, December 2011.

7. That's because there is scant evidence that preventive care lowers costs. As I go over at length in a later chapter, preventive care may sometimes improve long-term health prospects, but it almost never reduces total healthcare costs due to costly upfront screenings that exceed long-run cost savings. Even worse, preventive care actually makes long-term health prospects worse in some cases, due to misdiagnosis and overtreatment.

8. Please do not confuse health savings accounts (HSAs) with medical savings accounts (MSAs). HSAs are long-term savings vehicles, whereas any money deposited into an MSA evaporates at the end of each year. MSAs are tools by which employers can provide short-term healthcare-related fringe benefits, like annual stipends to purchase eyeglasses.

9. Buying solo is more expensive because insurance companies are worried about adverse selection problems and the likelihood that most people applying one-at-a-time for individual policies will be sickly rather than healthy, and therefore prone to running up costs. The most common solution to this problem is to not allow people to purchase insurance one-at-a-time, but rather to offer insurance only to large, predefined groups (such as all of the workers at a large firm). By offering group coverage, insurance companies know people won't be able to sort themselves into or out of plans based on how healthy they are. High-deductible health insurance plans reassure insurance companies about adverse selection problems in a different way. Only healthy people are likely to select high-deductible plans (since they know they will be 100 percent responsible for all spending up to the amount of the high deductible). Thus, insurance companies can offer low premiums because the insurance pool is likely dominated by healthy people who won't run up a lot of costs.

10. Mitch Daniels, "Hoosiers and Health Savings Accounts," *Wall Street Journal*, March 1, 2010, https://www.wsj.com/articles/ SB10001424052748704231304575091600470293066.
11. Remember that I am using Singaporean terminology here for the word "copay." This 20 percent "copay" is what most American healthcare experts would refer to as a 20 percent "co-insurance" rate.

Chapter 22: RAND and Oregon: Slashing Spending without Hurting Health

1. The six were Dayton, Ohio; Seattle, Washington; Fitchburg and Franklin Counties in Massachusetts; and Charleston and Georgetown Counties in South Carolina.
2. The statistical method for doing this is known as "instrumental variables." To understand how it works, consider this simplified version of the Oregon experiment. Suppose you start with two hundred people enrolling for one hundred lottery spots that would allow them to apply for Medicaid. One hundred win the lottery and one hundered don't. Then, of the one hundred who win the lottery, suppose only twenty-five end up enrolled in Medicaid. We can then compare a health outcome—say systolic blood pressure—between the one hundred who won the lottery and the one hundred who didn't. Suppose that systolic blood pressure averages 125 among those who won the lottery and 126 among those who lost the lottery. Since there was a lottery, the demographics of the two groups should be, on average, equal. So we can assume that the only reason that there is a one-point difference between the two groups in terms of systolic blood pressure is because twenty-five of the lottery winners got to enroll and benefit from Medicaid whereas zero of the lottery losers got to enroll or benefit from Medicaid. That is, all the differences can be ascribed to the subgroup of twenty-five lottery winners who ended up receiving Medicaid. There was a one-point difference in systolic blood pressure on average between the one hundred lottery winners and the one hundred

lottery losers—but at the same time, that difference can only be ascribed to the twenty-five lottery winners who actually received Medicaid. It therefore must be the case that going on Medicaid causes a four-point difference in systolic blood pressure (which looks like only a one-point difference when you compare the one hundred lottery winners with the one hundred lottery losers, because the twenty-five lottery winners who benefited from Medicaid are only one-fourth of the total number of one hundred lottery winners, all of whom collectively have systolic blood pressure that is one point lower than lottery losers).

3. Katherine Baicker et al, "The Oregon Experiment—Effects of Medicaid on Clinical Outcomes," *New England Journal of Medicine* 368 (2013): 1713–22.

4. Amy Finkelstein et al., "The Oregon Health Insurance Experiement: Evidence from the First Year," *Quarterly Journal of Economics* 127 no. 3 (2012): 1057–106.

5. Sarah Taubman et al., "Medicaid Increases Emergency Department Use: Evidence from Oregon's Health Insurance Experiment," *Science* 343 no. 6168 (2014): 263–68.

Chapter 23: Why Healthcare Spending Can Decline without Hurting Health Outcomes

1. John P. Bunker, "The role of medical care in contributing to health improvements within societies," *International Journal of Epidemiology* 30, Issue 6 (December 1, 2001): 1260–63.

2. Godias J. Drolet and Anthony M. Lowell, "A Half-Century's Progress Against Tuberculosis in New York City 1900–1950,"(New York: New York Tuberculosis and Health Association, 1952). Mimeograph, https://www1.nyc.gov/html/doh/downloads/pdf/tb/tb1900.pdf.

3. New York City Department of Health and Mental Hygiene, 2011, "Summary of Vital Statistics 2010 The City of New York."

4. David M. Cutler and Grant Miller, "The Role of Public Health Improvements in Health Advances: The Twentieth-Century United States," *Demography* 42, Issue 1 (2005): 1–22.

5. Environmental Protection Agency,"Water on Tap: What you Need to Know," 2009.

6. FE Andre et al., "Vaccination greatly reduces disease, disability, death and inequity worldwide," Bulletin of the World Health Organization 86, no. 2(2008): 81–160.

7. Gerald F. Riley and James D. Lubitz, "Long-Term Trends in Medicare Payments in the Last Year of Life," *Health Services Research* 45, no. 2 (2010): 565–76.

8. LT Krogsboll et al., "General health checks in adults for reducing morbidity and mortality from disease: Cochrane systematic review and meta-analysis," *British Medical Journal* 345 e7191 (2012).

Michael Maciosek et al., "Greater Use of Preventive Services In US Health Care Could Save Lives at Little or No Cost," *Health Affairs* 29, no. 9 (2010): 1656–60.

9. Since childhood immunizations provide about 79 percent of the potential life extension benefits, the other nineteen provide about 21 percent. Take 21 percent of the 2 million additional life years that the authors calculate the twenty services would collectively generate if utilization rates were raised to 90 percent. That gives you only 420,000 additional life years (which can be interpreted as 420,000 people getting one extra year of life). Divide those 420,000 extra life years by the 2,515,548 people who died in 2013 to see that the 420,000 extra life years (if they had been distributed equally among all the people who died in 2013) would have given each deceased person an average of 0.167 extra years of life each. What does 0.167 extra years of life come out to? Sixty-one extra days.

Chapter 24: P, Q, and Big Savings for You

1. T. Campbell, D.U. Himmelstein, and S. Woolhandler, "Costs of health care administration in the United States and Canada," *New England Journal of Medicine* 349, no. 8, (2003): 768–75.

2. The Henry J. Kaiser Family Foundation, "Number of Retail Prescription Drugs Filled at Pharmacies by Payer," State Health Facts 2017, http://kff.org/other/state-indicator/total-retail-rx-drugs/.

3. Steven Findlay, "When You Should Go to an Urgent Care or Walk-In Health Clinic," *Consumer Reports*, May 4, 2018, http://www.consumerreports.org/cro/2013/01/urgent-care-what-you-need-to-know/index.htm.

4. The data includes all the actual prices charged to all CareFirst BlueCross BlueShield members in 2013 by urgent care centers and emergency rooms. Please note that average prices given in the study are not only for emergency rooms and urgent care centers but also for convenient care clinics, which charge even less than urgent care centers. But because urgent care centers are more common than convenient care clinics, I chose to give only price comparisons between emergency rooms and urgent care centers. As convenient care clinics proliferate, though, there will be even greater opportunities for savings relative to emergency rooms than are indicated by my comparisons between ER prices and urgent-care prices. See: https://member.carefirst.com/individuals/managing-health-care-costs/er-versus-urgent-care-doctors-office-settings.page.

5. 2014 Urgent Care Benchmarking Survey Results, Urgent Care Association of America, http://www.ucaoa.org.

6. Centers for Medicare & Medicaid Services, "Hospital Compare" data listed under the "Timely and Effective Care" data, https://data.medicare.gov/Hospital-Compare/Timely-and-Effective-Care-Hospital/yv7e-xc69.

7. *Global Health and Travel*, July–August 2013, 56. Please note that all prices were converted into US dollars to make price comparisons straightforward. Also note that these prices are

the full-freight prices charged to foreigners. Locals can usually get even lower prices with government subsidies that are available only to citizens and residents (such as Singapore's direct subsidies system).

8. Singapore Ministry of Manpower, "Table: Occupational Wage, 2013," June 30, 2014, http://stats.mom.gov.sg/Pages/Occupational-Wages-Tables-2013.aspx.

9. The US Bureau of Labor Statistics' *Occupational Outlook Handbook* lists the 2012 median total compensation of US primary care physicians at $220,942 and that of physicians practicing in medical specialties at $396,223. See http://www.bls.gov/ooh/healthcare/physicians-and-surgeons.htm#tab-5. More recent comparisons of primary care and specialist earnings in Singapore vs. the United States are not available because the Singapore Ministry of Manpower currently publishes only *specialist* physician median earnings (S$260,748 in 2017), while the United States Bureau of Labor Statistics currently publishes only *general practitioner* median earnings ($208,560 in 2017).

Chapter 25: You Have to Fund People's HSAs for Them

1. Abby Goodnough and Robert Pear, "Unable to Meet the Deductible or The Doctor," *New York Times*, October 17, 2014; Tom Howell Jr., "One in four Americans who got insurance still can't afford medical care: Study," *Washington Times*, May 14, 2015.

2. Sara R Collins et al., "Too High a Price: Out-of-Pocket Health Care Costs in the United States," findings from the Commonwealth Fund Health Care Affordability Tracking Survey, September–October 2014, November 13, 2014, http://www.commonwealthfund.org/publications/issue-briefs/2014/nov/out-of-pocket-health-care-costs.

Chapter 26: We Must Rescue the Poor from Medicaid

1. Joseph Kwok et al., "The Impact of Health Insurance Status on the Survival of Patients with Head and Neck Cancer," *Cancer* 116 no. 2 (2010): 476–85.

2. Damien J. LaPar et al., "Primary Payer Status Affects Mortality for Major Surgical Operations," *Annals of Surgery* 252 no. 3 (September 2010): 544–51.

3. Michael A. Gaglia Jr. et al., "Effect of Insurance Type on Adverse Cardiac Events After Percutaneous Coronary Intervention," *American Journal of Cardiology* 107, no. 5 (March 2011): 675–80.

4. Jeremiah G. Allen et al., "Insurance status is an independent predictor of long-term survival after lung transplantation in the United States," *Journal of Heart and Lung Transplantation* 30, no. 1 (January 2011): 45–53.

5. Decker, Sandra L, "In 2011, Nearly One-Third of Physicians Said They Would Not Accept New Medicaid Patients, But Rising Fees May Help," *Health Affairs*, 31, no. 8 (August 2012), 1673–79.

6. J. Bisgaier and KV Rhodes, "Auditing Access to Specialty Care for Children with Public Insurance," *New England Journal of Medicine* 364, no. 24, (June 2011): 2324–33.

7. Thankfully, the waiver denial that was alluded to in the title of the article was later reversed. The Healthy Indiana Program continues to serve Indiana's poor. For more information, see Avik Roy, "Obama Administration Denies Waiver for Indiana's Popular Medicaid Program," *Forbes*, November 11, 2011, https://www.forbes.com/sites/aroy/2011/11/11/obama-administration-denies-waiver-for-indianas-popular-medicaid-reform/#25f448443ff0.

8. Ibid.

Chapter 27: Visiting the Free Market Medical Association

1. When a company negotiates traditional health insurance for its employees, the insurance contract will specify which doctors

are covered and which are not. The result is an automatic flow of covered patients to "in-network" providers. Those in-network providers do not need to worry about cultivating or maintaining any of those relationships to maintain their flow of covered patients.

2. The price tag was invented by John Wanamaker, a retail marketing genius who built the first department store in Philadelphia, invented the price tag, and then also invented the money-back guarantee. In Chapter 28, you will read more about Mr. Wannamaker and why the price tag is so important for reforming the US healthcare system.

Chapter 28: My Proposal for Reforming the US Healthcare System

1. Austin Frakt, "Price Transparency Is Nice. Just Don't Expect It to Cut Health Costs," *New York Times,* December 19, 2016.
2. This is true because Provider A could point out not only his own price, but also the prices of every other competitor (since they would have to post their prices, too).

Chapter 29: Help Defeat the Special Interests

1. Center for Responsive Politics, https://www.opensecrets.org/lobby/top.php?indexType=i&showYear=a. Dollar figures are for the period January 1, 1998 through October 16, 2018.